Through Defeat to Victor

ALSO BY MORTON KELSEY

Tongue Speaking
God, Dreams and Revelation
Encounter with God
Healing and Christianity
Myth, History and Faith
The Christian and the Supernatural
The Other Side of Silence
Can Christians Be Educated?
The Cross
Discernment
Dreams
Tales to Tell
The Age of Miracles
Afterlife
Adventure Inward
Reaching for the Real
Caring
Transcend
Prophetic Ministry
Christo-Psychology
Companions on the Inner Way
Resurrection
Christianity as Psychology
Sacrament of Sexuality
Psychology, Medicine and Christian Healing
Reaching: The Journey to Fulfillment
Prayer and the Redwood Seed

MORTON KELSEY

Through Defeat to Victory

Stories and Meditations of Spiritual Rebirth

ELEMENT

Rockport, Massachusetts ● Shaftesbury, Dorset

© 1991 Morton Kelsey

Published in the U.S.A. in 1991 by Element, Inc.
42 Broadway, Rockport, MA 01966

Published in Great Britain in 1991 by Element
Books Limited, Longmead, Shaftesbury, Dorset

Cover design by Max Fairbrother
Text design by Roger Lightfoot
Typeset by Burns and Smith Ltd, Derby
Printed in the United States of America
by Edwards Brothers Inc.

Library of Congress Data available

British Library Cataloguing in Publication Data

Kelsey, Morton (Morton Trippe), *1917*–
    Through defeat to victory: stories and
    meditations of spiritual rebirth.
    I. Title
    248.34

ISBN 1–85230–270–4

To my friend, Andy Canale,
who has helped me and many others
to find the resurrection victory
on the other side of defeat.

Contents

Introduction   1

PART ONE: THE STORIES   9

1. How It All Began   11
2. Alice Maywell   17
3. Eric Adams   22
4. Edith Rankin   27
5. Norma Carter   32
6. Edna Masters   36
7. The Reverend Alfred Darby   40
8. James Donally   45
   Epilogue to Part One   50

PART TWO: THE MEDITATIONS   54

Introduction   55
1. What Happened at the First Easter?   57
2. Letting God In   63
3. Listening   68
4. Patience and Knowing God   74
5. Righting Wrongs with Christ   79
6. Why Evil in God's World?   84
7. To Love, To Console   90
8. What Is Heaven Like?   96
9. The Practical Importance of Heaven   101
10. He Is Risen, Alleluia!   109
    Epilogue to Part Two   114

Introduction

One theme runs through the Gospel narrative much as a musical theme runs through a symphony and gives it unity. The Gospel melody is not one that most humans like to hear. It sings that we find life by giving it up! We find victory on the other side of defeat. The message is clear: astonishing and eternal victory is available, but it is not easily attained. Indeed, it is found most often on the other side of brokenness, defeat, despair, and after we have given up our will.

Jesus taught this message, preached it, and lived it. He was born of poor parents under very questionable circumstances. He spent his first years as a refugee in a hostile land. When he began his ministry, he was rejected by the people of his own town and his own family. He lived among the outcasts, the tax collectors, the prostitutes—those who did not follow the law. The lepers and the sick, thought to be suffering from divine punishment for their sins, came to him and he healed them. After a brief time of popularity, he was rejected and condemned by the leaders of his own church and he fled to foreign territory. He spoke to one who wanted to follow him: "Birds have nests and foxes have holes, but the Son of Man has no place to lay his head."

Finally he entered the Holy City at the Passover and confronted the religious leaders by driving the money changers, and those who bought and sold there, out of the temple. He was betrayed by one of his own disciples, brought bound to the Sanhedrin, condemned, and turned over to Pontius Pilate. He was mocked, beaten, crucified between two thieves, and died. He cried out from the cross: "My God, my God, why have you forsaken me?"

His defeat was complete, but it was not the end of the story as it should have been from a human point of view. Something happened. Broken, terror-stricken friends and disciples were suddenly transformed and went out into the world preaching the Good News that there can be victory on the other side of hopeless defeat. And what changed them? They said that Jesus had risen from the dead and appeared to them transformed, transcendent, glorified. These men and women not only spoke this conviction, they witnessed it with their lives. They did not waver in their hope even when they were struck down just like their master had been. Others took their places and the movement of the followers of Jesus grew in spite of persecution and defeat. Within three hundred years nearly half the people of the Roman Empire had become Christians.

We can look at the inhumanity of people for each other and give up in anguish or we can look up through it and hope for victory. Sometimes when we are experiencing the very heart of darkness, we are visited by the very presence of victory—the Risen One. When Stephen was being stoned, he saw the heavens opened and the Risen One at the right hand of God. In 1660 James Nayler's last words after disgrace and brutal attack were these:

> There is a spirit which I feel that delights to do no evil, nor to revenge any wrong, but delights to endure all things, in hope to enjoy its own in the end. Its hope is to outlive all wrath and contention, and to weary out all exaltation and cruelty, or whatever is of a nature contrary to itself . . . I found it alone, being forsaken. I have fellowship therein with them who lived in dens and desolate places in the earth, who through death obtained this resurrection and eternal holy life.

Several years ago at a conference, a woman wrote an account of a brutal attack by three men when she was nine years old. She was close to death and torn between desires to live or die. A voice spoke to her and told her she must make her decision soon or she would be dead. It then told her to move her legs. She couldn't move a muscle and then she saw the luminous figure of the Risen One who stooped down and moved her leg for her. One of the men saw that she was still alive, took pity upon her, and took her home.

Transformations like these are historical facts. It is strange how few modern theologians want to deal with the historical facticity of Jesus' resurrection. In his remarkable study *The Resurrection of Jesus: A Jewish Perspective*, Pinchas Lapide pokes fun at Christian thinkers who want to put a "dogmatic curtain between the pre-Easter and the risen Jesus in order to protect the latter against any contamination of earthly three dimensionality." He then states that for the first Christians "the immediate historicity was not only a part of that happening but the indispensable precondition for the recognition of its significance for salvation." In his remarkable book *World Religions*, Huston Smith in his discussion of Christianity makes the same point clearly and eloquently.

This resurrection is so much more than an affirmation of life beyond death. I find that most people are not touched by Easter's victory unless they have experienced defeat, rejection, tragedy. Those who have suffered and have lost all hope can find in the condemned, rejected, defeated Jesus one who understands the worst of the human condition. They can identify with him. They are no longer totally alone and forsaken. And even if they do not know much about the resurrection and have not reflected upon it, they know that Jesus' crucifixion would not still be honored if this torture had simply snuffed out a person whom most agree was one of the finest human beings known to history.

The crucifixion and resurrection are inextricably intertwined. Crucifixion without resurrection is the victory of evil, bigotry, torture, war, hatred, and fear. Resurrection without crucifixion is a bright hope most often beyond our grasp. The two together speak of evil and violence overcome, transformed. Together they enable us to look at the darkest corners of our own souls and to deal with the oppression, poverty, and misery that surround us in our broken world. In James Russell Lowell's hymn, the cross and resurrection are portrayed as two aspects of one event.

> Though the cause of evil prosper,
> Yet 'tis truth alone is strong.
> Though his portion be the scaffold,
> And upon the throne is wrong.
> Yet that scaffold sways the future,
> And, behind the dim unknown,
> Standeth God within the shadow
> Keeping watch above their own.

The fresco "The Mystery of Faith" by Ben Long IV, expresses the same truth so powerfully that I used it for the cover of my book *Resurrection, Release from Oppression.*

The crucifixion–resurrection are the two central acts of the cosmic drama of Christianity. The first act is described in the Old Testament and tells of a nation seeking to find the one God, parent to all humankind. But there is no solution to the problem of evil as the story of Job reveals. Creation at that point is incomplete. There is no suffering savior who knows our weakness and pleads for us. We find hints of such a figure there, but no victorious redeemer, no one to vindicate us.

God sees the hopelessness of the human plight and in the fullness of time God puts off divine power and becomes a human being—a fragile human child—and lives among the oppressed in an occupied country. He begins to preach and teach and heal. By the stories he told and lived, he reveals that God is a loving Abba who wishes to draw all human beings to that love. And those who wish to come are asked only to express the same kind of love toward all other human beings that Abba gives to them. Abba is like the father of the prodigal and receives the lost one back and pours out showers of gifts upon him, and then goes off to plead with the self-righteous elder brother to come into the feast. Jesus told the story of the prodigal and then he lived it through the crucifixion–resurrection to demonstrate the reality of his story.

Then Jesus leaves his disciples in a blaze of light. Yet they are not sad, for though Jesus is no longer physically present, they have not lost him. The barriers between heaven and earth have broken down. One from our time might well have expressed this last of the great resurrection appearances in the words of Howard Chandler Robbins:

> The heaven that hides him from our sight
> Knows neither near nor far;
> An altar candle sheds its light
> As surely as a star;
> And where his loving people meet
> To share the gift divine,
> There stands he with unhurrying feet;
> There heavenly splendors shine.

The infinitely loving Abba has become infinitely available.

Then, the spirit of Abba is poured out upon those who will receive it. All people can be carriers of the divine, of the Holy Spirit—not just the prophets and seers—but all humankind. And so humans now share in the very nature of God. Even the lost and broken, when touched by this Spirit, have access to the kingdom of heaven and can share the knowledge and power of that kingdom with other human beings.

The last act of the cosmic drama depends on us. Will we become ambassadors of this kingdom? Will we come to know the love of God, let it penetrate to the depth of our own being and then share it with others, and particularly the forgotten and the broken, the lost and the poor? God wants to take us into partnership with Love.

This God to whom we turn is far more than just masculine or feminine. The Holy One is both our mother and our father. In many biblical images the Divine is viewed as the mother hen wishing to take her chicks under her wings or as the incredibly loving and caring prodigal father. This eternal creator combines the quality of both mother and father. We have no word in English to express this reality, and when he is used in quotations we understand it as this divine reality.

This book deals with both of the two central acts of the cosmic drama. The first part addresses the problem of human suffering in the light of Jesus' terrible crucifixion. A group of hurting people found transformation and victory as they paused for several hours on Good Friday listening to and meditating upon the account of the crucifixion. Jesus' awesome and courageous death on a cross can strike deeply into our hearts when we really look at it. The Negro spiritual expresses the essence of what Jesus' death meant to an enslaved people: "Were you there when they crucified my Lord?"

The second part of the book looks at the victory of the resurrection of Jesus and what this victory means for our lives. Here, we offer meditations so that we may assimilate more of the unfathomable meaning of the incredible victory that was won for humankind by the dual event of Jesus' crucifixion-resurrection.

The Importance of Stories

Stories tell much more than logical discussions. The stories that follow are true stories about human transformation. They tell of people who found victory on the other side of defeat. Transformation occurred in them as they looked at their own pain and hopelessness in the light of the cross and resurrection and shared with each other what they found. They would never have looked at the crucifixion if it had led only to death and meaningless annihilation. They were not, however, caught up by the victory of the resurrection. That was beyond them. They were caught up by the nobility of this human being, Jesus of Nazareth, as he suffered and died. They watched with him and listened to the words he spoke as he suffered there and something changed them. Sharing the pain of other human beings is easier for most of us than sharing in their joy and experiences of transcendence.

Not all of us find God in this dramatic way. Some find the presence of God in quietness as they wait for the dazzling darkness. Perhaps they have not been wounded so deeply and they share more easily in the beauty of God's world. They have probably known the security of human love and have a quiet confidence that all will be well. But there are those of us who have been so wounded that we need to have a savior who can understand our brokenness and pain. We need one who knows our despair and could cry out: "My God, my God, why have you forsaken me?" Through the agony of Jesus and then his victory, we can begin to catch a glimpse of hope and light. This message of hope spoke to the slaves in the Roman Empire—three-fifths of the entire population. The cross of Christ still speaks directly to those overwhelmed by misery, oppression, loneliness, depression, and despair.

Jesus knew the worst of human agony and pain. Even those who are free of personal suffering can look out over the continents of earth and see the cruelty and sickness, the poverty and suffering of humans everywhere. One question comes to me more often in my lecturing than any other: "Why is there so much pain and suffering in a world created and sustained by a loving parent?"

There was a time when some Christians almost gloried in their suffering. Some even inflicted physical and mental pain on themselves so they could identify more with Christ's suffering.

When we truly know the depth of our own being, we usually find within us enough darkness and pain to deal with. We need seek no more. In forty years of counseling, I have discovered that nearly everyone carries a very heavy burden. Human kindness helps us with this suffering, but it does not solve the problem of evil in our world.

Among the great religions of this world, only Christianity speaks directly to the agony of the human condition. Many of the religions of the East suggest that our physical lives are illusion. As we become enlightened, we rise beyond this illusory world and its ugliness. In the West, secular thinkers from Freud to Sartre tell us stoically to bear an absurd and meaningless existence.

There is no logical answer to this problem of evil, but Jesus Christ and Christianity give us a practical solution. Evil and suffering are real. Jesus met them and conquered them. He gives us a way to overcome them with him. How victoriously the early Christians heard and lived this solution. Persecution and death in the arena did not defeat them. They knew the victory of Jesus on the cross and they shared it.

I have discovered that modern men and women can be touched by the same victory and share in it. How can we pass on this incredibly vital and encouraging message? Theological language often leaves us untouched. Stories and meditations, however, reach beyond our rational minds and move the heart and emotions.

Jesus taught in stories and parables. In my book *The Other Side of Silence*, I show how story and imagination can be used to bring us into a vital relationship with the victorious Christ. In another book, *The Cross*, I have stepped back in imagination to the crucifixion itself and looked at the power it exerted on those who actually watched Jesus die on the cross.

One of the incomparable gifts of the Eucharist is that it allows us to celebrate both Jesus' death and resurrection. In this liturgy, we participate in Jesus' suffering, death, and victory. The church reenacts the drama of salvation in this central service of Christendom and drama is story in action.

Jesus told stories of the kingdom of heaven. He lived the same story in his life and death and resurrection. He instituted the Eucharist so we could continue to live in that story.

In Part One stories of seven people are told so that *The Story* may become more real to us. They are modern parables about suffering men and women who were touched by the cross of Christ and found victory on the other side of defeat. They are composite stories from actual victories which I have seen take place in forty years as a pastor, teacher, and counselor. Lives were saved from chaos as the cross became a vital symbol to seeking human beings.

Suffering, war, poverty, oppression, and slavery are real and sometimes we can with courage be transformed in the midst of disaster. However, as Paul Tournier has pointed out, for every three hundred who grow through intense suffering, several million are destroyed. We are not glorifying or minimizing pain and suffering. What I am saying is that I know of no other true comfort in terrible affliction than the cross of Christ. He won a victory for us there and so gives us a victory over evil and suffering if not here, in the immeasurable and mysterious vistas of eternity. *However, once we have known that victory over suffering and evil is possible, one of our greatest obligations is to do all we can to transform the social and political structures that grind human beings into dust and to eliminate the physical suffering of disease and loneliness.* Many of those who have made the greatest impact on human suffering have been those who were touched by the victory of the cross and then went out to heal our broken world.

I first wrote this introduction at a time when my life was brought to a screeching stop. I could no longer run my life as I wished. I had to give up my way of life and follow a way I did not wish to go. I had written these composite stories many years before when I first learned that there was a way through darkness to light, through defeat to victory. Like so many important insights, I find that I now have to learn them again and again.

Gualala, California
Holy Week 1991

Part One: The Stories

Fellowship in Victory Over Defeat

Oh risen Jesus, through your life-giving death,
enable us by your Spirit to pass through our
defeats victoriously and then reach out to other
fragile human beings with the message of
hope—the hope that beyond the darkness we
may not only find light, but the transforming
brilliance of eternity. We ask this of you who
knew our misery, came among us, suffered
with us, suffered for us and threw wide the
portals of eternal life for us. Amen.

1   How It All Began

From the beginning of the service Calvary Church had been crowded with people. The church was stripped and bare for the occasion. The eight meditations were interspersed with times of quiet and prayer. Perhaps more people were there on this particular Good Friday because a life-sized cross, built of secondhand lumber, stood on the busy boulevard to call people to stop a moment and think, to drop their busyness and be still.

The minister's meditations were not particularly inspired, but they were honest and sincere. He incorporated large sections of scripture as he told the story of the first Good Friday. He explained simply and directly the force of each of the words Jesus had uttered on the cross. He started with the Last Supper these men had shared together, in which they broke bread and blessed wine and pledged their faithfulness. Judas left when the Passover meal was finished and it was night. Then, taking up torches and singing hymns, the Master and his friends made their way out of Jerusalem to the safety of the Garden of Gethsemane. The Master was in spiritual agony and he asked several of his disciples to come apart with him and watch while he prayed; the rest were to watch farther down the hill. But they were all very tired; the weight of the things that were to come was too heavy, and so they slipped into the unconsciousness of sleep while the Master sweated great drops of blood. He came back and found them sleeping and asked them to watch again. How much he needed some human fellowship that night, but they went to sleep again.

Then he woke them. The soldiers were upon them, and Judas came up and kissed the Master and said, "Hail, Master!" and Jesus replied, "Friend, why are you here?" Then the soldiers seized Jesus, for the kiss had been the sign. A brief fracas ensued; a few swords were brandished and the disciples fled into the dark Judean night. Laughing and mocking, the Temple guard pushed the man down the pathway toward the Temple grounds where the Sanhedrin met. There some of the elders of the people had gathered in expectation and a farce of a trial took place. . . . False witnesses had been secured who accused Jesus of Nazareth of the most awful blasphemies. The verdict was a foregone conclusion, and when it was pronounced they blindfolded him and buffeted him and told him to prophesy which of them had hit him, and they laughed. All this time Peter had waited outside in the courtyard only to deny his Master three times. . . .

As the cock crowed, they took him to Pilate, for they could not carry out the death penalty themselves. They accused the man of seeking to set up a new kingdom, but Pilate was no fool. He saw through them, and in order to release Jesus, he sent him to Herod Antipas who had authority over Galileans, but Herod only played with him before his courtesans and sent him back to Pilate. Again Pilate tried to free Jesus of Nazareth and he announced that, according to custom, one of the prisoners might be freed. Which would the crowd have? The crowd cried, "Barabbas." Pilate asked them what should be done with Jesus who is called the Christ and the mob, egged on by the priests, cried out all the more violently, "Crucify him! Crucify him!" Then Pilate took water and washed his hands and listened to his wife speak of a bad dream she had had concerning this man, but, giving in to the pressure of the Temple authorities, he delivered him to be crucified. . . .

The soldiers took him to the praetorium where they stripped him and flogged him. Then they made sport of him and placed a purple cloak about him and did mocking obeisance to him, saying, "Hail, King of the Jews." They plaited a crown of thorns for him, forced it upon his head, struck him with a reed, and spat on him, and then they led him forth to crucify him. His strength failed as he carried the heavy crossbar up the hill of Golgotha, the place of the skull, and a bystander, a black man, Simon of Cyrene, was dragged from the watching crowd to carry it for him.

Arriving at Golgotha, they offered him wine mingled with gall to drink, but he refused it. They stripped him, laid him upon the crossbar, drove the nails through the fine strong palms, and then lifted him to the upright which stood waiting and nailed his feet to it. They crucified him between two thieves. Their task done, the soldiers sat down at the foot of the cross to gamble for his clothes and wait for them to die.

The two thieves cursed and screamed, but Jesus uttered no word until some hours later when he looked around at the soldiers and the priests, the indifferent jeering mob, and the few faithful friends and said, "Father, forgive them for they know not what they do."

Half an hour passed and he spoke again, this time in answer to a request. The thieves, who were being crucified with him, had made fun of him at first, reviling and taunting him, but gradually one of them fell silent. There was something more than human in this man dying there beside him, and he cried out, "Jesus, remember me when you come into your kingly power," and the Master turned his head toward him and gave him the most sweeping kind of forgiveness that anyone could seek, saying, "Truly I say to you, today you will be with me in paradise."

Another half hour or so passed and Jesus looked down on his mother and beloved disciple standing at the foot of the cross and said, "Mother, behold your son," and turning to his friend, "Son, behold your mother." In these brief words he told them to go on, to cherish the common family bonds, to continue them, to be faithful to them . . . all was not over or lost.

Then he uttered the most terrible cry. As the sun disappeared behind the clouds, Jesus, in despair and agony and separated from humans and from God, cried out, *"Eloi, Eloi, lama sabachthani.* . . . My God, my God, why have you forsaken me!" And then his body's agony welled forth as the traumatic thirst, the thirst of the wounded, forced from him the cry, "I thirst." A young priest came and filled a sponge with wine and lifted it to his lips and he drank.

Life was ebbing from him as he spoke the last two times. He uttered a strange statement, often misunderstood: "It is finished." He spoke this to himself. His task was complete, brought to fulfillment, to perfection; it was finished. These were words of victory, not defeat. Then he spoke to the Father. With confidence and trust he spoke these final words: "Father, into your hands I commend my spirit." Then he uttered a great cry and gave up the ghost. The soldiers thrust a spear into his side and Joseph of Arimathea took down his body and buried it in a tomb nearby.

The minister completed the story. The meditations were over. The soloist sang. The plaintive words and the minor melody died away. . . . "Were you there when they laid him in the tomb?" A heavy hush fell upon the church, a deep quiet. . . . The bell tolled—slowly one peal followed another. Thirty-three times the bell tolled. Then the silence of the politely attentive congregation broke as the people began to stir and move toward the door. Quietly the people slipped out and the church emptied. The minister was not at the door to greet the people. Without speaking even to their friends, the people went to their cars and their homes. . . .

Most of the people had been touched by the service, though their lives would not be noticeably changed, but scattered within the church there lingered a handful of people. They were hardly aware that the service was over. . . . They did not realize that the others were gone. They were deep within themselves. Something new had opened for them and they gazed intently upon the new vistas of an inner world, oblivious of the outer one. A door had opened for them between these worlds.

The minister returned to turn out the lights. It had been a gray, gloomy day, dark and threatening. He saw them there, the seven of them. He knew none of them. They were all strangers. His first impulse was to turn off the lights and so invite them to leave, but something stopped him. He was tired. He was not the most religiously or spiritually developed person in the world, yet he could detect the reality of the Spirit of God when it was present, and the more he looked upon them the more awed he was. Something had happened in his church that day.

He sat down in the back of the church and watched. He could not help but smile at the seven people scattered there before him. They formed an incongruous group. There was a lady of middle age in a magnificent mink cape. Resting on her head was a hat of exquisite taste. Her bearing was one of easy elegance and power, the kind that comes from many years of directing others, and yet her face was streaked and her eyes were red. . . . Even now her frame was shaken with an occasional repressed sob, but strangely there was actually an air of release and joy about her. . . .

Sitting next to her was one of indeterminate age, as different as one could imagine. She wore no hat at all, and her hair had not seen a comb or brush in many days. Her unironed dress hung carelessly upon her bony frame. From where the minister sat, he saw nails that were black. She wore old and broken shoes on stockingless feet. There was an emptiness of expression about her face, and yet there was something else, a light of hope and expectancy quite different from her attire. In the last pew not far from the preacher sat a young man, not more than twenty-two or twenty-three. He wore a sports shirt, khaki slacks, and engineer's boots. He was powerfully built and his face spoke of bitterness and anger. There were heavy lines about his mouth and eyes. He sat staring, open-mouthed into space. Now and then his eyes would fall on the black-veiled cross, and he would bury his head in his hands.

The more the minister observed, the more moved he was. Such people as these seldom came to his church and seldom lingered long when they did come. He left his pew and walked quietly up toward the middle of the nave so that he could have a better look at the other four. These were not quite as strikingly different as those who hugged the back of the church. There was a man of early middle age in a rather garish plaid suit. His shoes were brightly shined and his clothes were immaculately pressed. An odd-colored tie, again rather extravagant, and a tinted shirt gave the impression of a man trying to be something that he was not. His hair was slicked back against his head, bright and lustrous. His face was rather blank, perhaps purposefully so. . . . He was deep in thought and noticed none of those around him. Once or twice he knitted his brows; a smile came to his face, and then he heaved a great sigh of relief. . . .

In front of him was a woman bent and deformed. The wooden pew of the church caused her real discomfort. She was dressed well, but plainly. The pain, which she had carried so long, told on her face. Her eyes were sunken and drab, her face sallow. Yet suffusing this deformed creature was a radiant spirit, almost a glow or aura. One could almost see the new life pouring through her.

Over by a pillar, far from the rest, was a truly stunning young woman; her grooming was fully equal to the beauty it heightened and her clothes spoke of Saks Fifth Avenue or Neiman-Marcus. She had natural poise. The minister had noticed her when he had been preaching—one could not fail to notice her. She had listened attentively to his every word and was the very soul of politeness to those for whom she had to move as the people came and went during the service. Yet there had been an agonizing lostness about her that her charm and grace emphasized. There had been a dryness in her, and now out of the desert of her soul a spring was breaking forth.

One more remained, a priest of the church. His black suit was threadbare and shabby. His vest was spotted and stained, and a crumpled gray felt hat lay beside him. There were but few unknown clergy in the vicinity of Calvary Church and the preacher had spotted him early in the service. He had come in before the service began. How tired he looked and worn, as if the burdens of the world were upon him. There had been no change in him until the very end of the service and then an amazing transformation had taken place. It was at the end of the sixth meditation that his eyes had suddenly brightened. He had taken a deep breath and smiled, and then he began to weep silently—they were tears of gratitude and thanksgiving.

For well over half an hour these people remained (silently) in the church and then the minister had an idea. One by one he went up to the people and sat with them and asked each of them to step across the street to the rectory and share a cup of coffee with him. Each one had accepted gratefully and soon the eight of them were gathered in the rectory living room. A fire blazed on the hearth.

At first the minister carried most of the conversation, but soon the charming young woman broke in, and then the lady in the mink cape. Quite naturally they all began to speak. They told seven amazing stories of how they happened to be in Calvary Church that Good Friday and what had happened to them. . . . Seven people had been transformed that afternoon as they paused to rethink and relive the events of Jesus' crucifixion so many years ago. . . . But, really there were eight, for the minister had never before realized the power of the faith he preached. Eight people made new friends that day, friendships that were to change their lives. . . . Seven people had faced utter defeat as they happened into Calvary that gloomy March afternoon and eight men and women found new hope.

2   Alice Maywell

"Father, forgive them
for they know not what
they do."

The lady in the mink cape had been the first one touched on that dark Good Friday at Calvary Church. Her name was Alice Maywell. She didn't know exactly why she had come to church that afternoon. She had been in church only a few times in her life. Going to church, as one of her friends had twittered, was "decent" in her set only for baptisms and weddings. As for God or Jesus, these words usually suggested that an oath was at hand. No, she was definitely not the religious type, and yet something had happened in church that afternoon . . . something so profound and wonderful that she could not believe what she heard Alice Maywell speaking.

Her life had been filled with every luxury that money could buy. Her father had started with one small grocery store and through hard work had made it into a large one. Soon it was the largest store in the small midwestern city in which they lived. Her father then started another store in a city a few miles away. He ended up with a chain of fifty stores and a fortune which made him a financial and political power in several states. At first her mother had been deeply interested in the business, but something happened between them, and then they went their separate ways—he in his business and she in her club work and social activities.

For their oldest child, a son, nothing was too good and the whirl of parties staged at their country estate was the talk of the entire state. Alice had been born to them late in life. She was sickly at birth and she remained so throughout her life. Her father gave one look at the sickly infant and growled to his wife that one could expect no better if one didn't take care of one's self. Her mother gave her a little love, just enough to keep her alive, and hired an Austrian maid to care for the child. She wanted to do better, but she had so much to do that she didn't have time.

The maids came and went, of course. They gave no sense of belonging, and Alice grew up the envy of the countryside, and yet a most unhappy and lonely little child. First she had her pony and then her horse, and then they sent her to the finest school in the East. Two events stood out in her memory. Coming home on the train, she had met her father in the dining car but he was so deep in business or politics that he did not even recognize her, or, if he did, he did not speak. The other was even more cruel. She had saved from her allowance and purchased a really beautiful picture for her mother for Christmas, only to find a year later that her mother had given it away as a present to a young chauffeur upon whom she doted.

When her father died, burned out at fifty, he was perfectly fair. Alice almost wished that he had not been. There was enough money in trust to give her an income of more than one hundred thousand dollars a year. At twenty she was completely independent. She decided to live her life exactly as she pleased. She took an apartment, first in Chicago and then New York, and began to travel wherever her heart desired. A few years later her mother died in an accident, and Alice found her income doubled.

She tried all the popular remedies for unhappiness—large cars, servants, beautiful homes, trips, even marriage. Each of these was as miserable a failure as the other. She found that most of her friends were looking to her for favors rather than wishing to give real understanding. Even her husband had his eye on her money far more than on her loveliness and tried to swindle her out of part of her fortune; she caught him at it and they were divorced. Now she was alone. She trusted no one. She had no reason to.

So, in desperation, she turned to the last popular remedy for unhappiness, the bottle. For the last ten years she had not been sober very often. Her money wrapped her in soft wool and protected her from the shocks of reality. She was bitter and hateful. She blamed her family for what it had done to her, the world because it did not accept her, herself whom she could not tolerate. Indeed, at heart and core she could not abide herself— her own uselessness—for she looked upon herself unconsciously from the eyes of her selfish and indifferent parents. She could not forgive herself for making so little of her life.

Alice Maywell fled from one place to another. She had come to this area for the races. Her growing desperation and hate became more apparent to her. If she did not find some release, some happiness, she had made up her mind to end her life. And so, half drunk, she rode down the boulevard and noticed the life-sized cross and had the driver stop. "Is it nothing to you, all you that pass by? Is there any sorrow, like unto my sorrow?" These words on the bulletin board struck her and invited her to enter. She took a seat in the back of the church hardly knowing where she was or what to do. She knew so little of the Christian gospel that she hardly knew what happened this day or why so many people were gathered on a Friday afternoon.

The story unfolded before her. Her imagination was vivid and she could see him—the strong, virile young man, courageous and outspoken, and the joy and admiration of those who knew him. She could see him deserted by followers afraid of the Temple, turned upon by the religious leaders of his own people, abandoned by his disciples, betrayed by one friend and denied by another, the laughingstock of the Sanhedrin and Herod, the pawn of Pilate, the sport of the soldiers, and now hanging upon a cross. . . . She knew what he experienced. She had been upon a cross for fifty years, although she had taken much wine to forget it in the last decade and a half. She knew what this poor fellow went through—but he, not through any folly of his own, but because he was trying to live his life according to the deepest and best in him. This had provoked the anger of the religious authorities.

She, on the other hand, had come to where she was of her own choosing. She had had a dozen opportunities to change. Several real friends had tried to relate to her, but those who disagreed with her were soon rejected. Stubbornly, persistently she had refused to look for any good in the world or see any in herself. She had not allowed herself to love or care for others because she thought no one could care for her. She knew what he felt, this pain of crucifixion, but he was without blame. At least this one knew what she bore, even if no other knew. They would not now be worshipping him if he had simply died and that had been the end.

Then came the second meditation and she heard the unforgettable words. (Remember, she had never heard them before.) "Father, forgive them for they know not what they do." He spoke these words to all who were there that day. . . . He spoke them to the High Priest and to Pilate, to the indifferent crowd who hadn't been present to cheer for him and those who had cried, "Crucify him," to the soldiers who sported with him and nailed him to the wood, to the jeering, sickening crowd that turned out for such things. She had seen a public execution in China. To all of them he spoke these words. He spoke them even to her—to Alice Maywell, who had had many opportunities to discover hope and new life and who had gone her own way to self-hate and self-pity. . . .

There evidently was a Father to forgive, and here was one to offer the forgiveness. It came first as a little stirring breath of air within the closed tomb of her soul, this thought that she could be forgiven. Then it grew to a breeze and then to a rushing, mighty wind that swept through her. She could be forgiven, her parents could be forgiven for what had happened between them and for their indifference to her. As they were forgiven, then her own inner being, which they had not accepted, could be accepted by the one who forgave. So it dawned on her that she had worth and value, and she, too, could forgive the maids who had ignored or neglected her and the teachers in private schools who had punished her unjustly. She could forgive the friends who had betrayed her, the husband who had tried to defraud her, and those who had grown sick of her self-pity and plied her with another stiff drink.

It was strange how quickly the alcoholic stupor passed from her, and how soon she saw things clearly, just as they were. She was a child of infinite worth and value and meaning. She heard few of the other words that were spoken. She was remembering, feeling through the past, receiving forgiveness, and giving it. She thought of the many who had tried to be kind whom she had turned away, of the young man who had tried to show her that he cared and whom she had laughingly rejected, of the one servant who had really given of herself to her. No, her life wasn't as bad as it might have been and, what was best of all, it was not too late. She still lived, and with this fresh hard ground upon which she now stood, she could make a new beginning. She did not have to end it all; she could begin a new life and she would. She wept honestly for the first time in years—tears of joy and freedom. She had a chance.

It was then that the minister had come to her and invited her to drop in for a cup of coffee. There she found others like herself. She could help this hardened young man to a new life, this broken woman who had sat beside her and whose odor had offended her, even the tortured priest.

I wish I could relate the whole of what happened after this, but that would be another story of her settling down in that little city, of caring for others, of finding and ministering to old friends, of looking out for the miserable and hungry and cold. How many cups of cool water she was to give. ''Inasmuch as you do it to one of these my brothers or sisters, you do it unto me.'' It took years, but she became what she dreamed she might, a new being with a rich, full life. His wounds had healed her hurt . . . and her hurt, as it was being healed, healed others. Out of suicidal despair, a new life was born. Hundreds of men and women were given new hope because she happened into church that day.

3　　Eric Adams

"Today you will
be with me
in paradise."

Eric Adams was no stranger to churches. He had been brought up in them from the time that he could walk. He had been a choirboy, had served at the altar, and had been active in religious organizations. For five years, however, he had not seen the inside of a church except for his mother's funeral.

From the outside, people admired his family, but seldom do people see behind the masks we erect for the public to view. His father was one of the officers of the local bank, and they lived in the best neighborhood in town in a spotless, white colonial house. They were not rich, but they had everything they required. Certainly there was never any need in his home. Eric had a paper route and then an after-school job with one of the merchants on the main street. These were to give him a sense of responsibility. The family enjoyed many outings together. His younger brother and sister, even now, were still at home and happy.

The trouble began when Eric was about fifteen and started to get ideas of his own, ideas of what he wanted to do and where he wanted to go. Up to this time there had been real affection and understanding, and then suddenly when he wanted to go his own way, to live his life in a way different from his parents, the great shock of his life came. His father would have nothing to do with him. Either he would do exactly what the father said or he would be on his own. To make matters even worse, his mother upon whom he had always leaned would not intercede for him. It came to him that she was really afraid of his father.

A conviction gradually grew in Eric's mind that interest and affection are given only for what the givers get out of them. He came to believe that there is no such thing as love that has no strings attached, no love that is not earned, but freely given and freely received. How little did he realize that his parents really feared that he might fall into the problems which had plagued them as teenagers. They were unconsciously trying to steer him clear of them. The effect, however, was the same as if they hadn't cared because they did not know how to relate, only to command.

As soon as he could, Eric left home. Since jobs were not easy to get and since he could not face returning home, he joined the army and was inducted. This was at the time of the police action in Korea and soon he found himself living under war conditions in an impoverished country torn by war and famine. He found himself with a type of person he had never dreamed existed, for he had been much overprotected and had very idealistic notions of what human beings were like. War brings out the most heroic elements in people, and also the basest. Eric saw only the latter, He could not bring himself to join some of the others in the evening sorties to the native village or be friends with those who did. He could not bring himself to let others know how he regarded such things, nor could he let them know how the feelings welled up within him for the starving children. He really thought that all real *men* were built of the pattern he had learned in high school, that they were all he-men with no feelings or sentiments, with no weaknesses in their impervious male armor.

It was then that the message came that his mother was very sick, but he could not obtain a leave to go home. He did not have the know-how or the influential friends. They did let him go when the message came that she was dead, but this was too late. Then he felt terribly guilty about his leaving home. He had not written home as he tried to punish his parents for their lack of understanding. He was in a daze as he flew home and the daze continued through the cold, formal funeral service.

The minister never came to call on the family. Eric went to see him in his office. He needed desperately to talk to someone. The minister listened to his story and said, ''Buck up, old man, with a fine church background like yours and a fine family you will pull yourself together in no time.'' This, of course, was just the advice he did not need and it was what he could not do. He went on home to find his father and his mother's brother in a terrible argument over some property left by his mother. He left the house, went to the Y, and then went back to his base. He tried to erase from his mind the happenings at home, in fact the home itself.

Back at the base he joined the boys and "tied one on." All of his pent-up animosities charged through him. He got into a mess and his partners in crime ratted on him to clear themselves. He was dishonorably discharged. When his money gave out, he began to steal. It did not bother him. He reasoned thus with himself, "No one does anything for anyone else because he wants to, but merely to get something out of them. All life is a racket. All business is a racket. The only difference between most occupations and crime is that crime is more honest and forthright in its facing what life is like. Since everyone is out for the other fellow's skin, why not go out for it openly and honestly and take what you want." He developed this mature criminal philosophy after he was discharged. He found a cheap room in a large, impersonal city.

Since Eric was reasonably clever, he went on for some months without getting caught. He found some companions in this new venture, and then the law caught up with him and he received a stiff sentence in the state prison. There he learned more finished techniques of crime and perfected his negative philosophy. And yet he found moments of depression, and he did not always sleep very well. He was determined, nonetheless.

He was released from prison on Maundy Thursday and fully intended to seek out his former companions and apply his new education. He rented a bed in a flophouse in a small city not far from the prison; then he put on a sport shirt and some khaki trousers and decided to case the town. As he walked down the boulevard, he passed the huge cross standing naked against the gray sky. He paused. Something old and forgotten was touched in him. Almost without his conscious mind knowing it, his feet were taking him into church. At the church he turned to leave, but the thought of doing this embarrassed him, and so he went on in and plunked himself down in the back pew.

What was it that the music stirred up in him? The old melodies set something nearly lost ringing in him. How he had been moved by these services when he was a youth. He had served as an acolyte at them and sat through the entire services. Then his conscious attitude came back and he laughed, and the look of scorn came back upon his face. He looked at the people sitting there. "Hypocrites," he muttered to himself under his breath. He looked at a well-dressed man and thought, "He is probably cheating his employees by paying poor wages." He looked at some young women there in a body from their office. "Suckers," was what his look conveyed.

The minister began to speak. He had not heard the story for a long time: Jesus Christ "betrayed," the word came again and again. Betrayed by his family, for they had thought him mad when first he began to preach and teach and heal, by his friends, by his government, by his church, betrayed, betrayed, betrayed. . . . He had never looked at Jesus in this light before. Here was one who had suffered exactly as he had, but how different was his response to his betrayal; instead of retribution and revenge, there had been patience, silence, forgiveness, endurance, and then resurrection.

How Eric had loved the glory of Easter—the brightness and joy after the gloom and ugliness of Good Friday. He shook his head to push these thoughts out, but he had opened a Pandora's box of old memories and they would not be pushed away. He remembered sitting through one of these services with his mother, who always brought a pencil and a pad so that he might scribble when he was restless. He remembered her warm and loving hand upon his shoulder. There was a tear in his eye as they sang the next hymn, "There's a Wideness in God's Mercy." Again he made an effort to push away these memories. The conflict was like a cross within his soul. Then, too, he told himself, Christ had spoken forgiveness to all those who had participated in his murder, but Christ couldn't forgive *him*. . . . Look at his record of ingratitude, anger, revenge, bitterness, crime . . . everything from rape to grand larceny. There was no hope for him.

Then the minister began to talk about the thief on the cross, how in the midst of his agony he had come to himself. After railing at Jesus, he had really begun to see the man who was dying there with him and he had the courage to say—for it takes great courage to admit that one is wrong, particularly under those circumstances—"Jesus, remember me when you come into your kingly power." He heard the minister give the words of reply, "Today you will be with me in paradise."

It was at this moment that Eric Adams came to himself. The minister showed how much like the story of the prodigal son was this scene between Jesus and the penitent thief. Eric saw

how his life had been that of the prodigal and here was the
father speaking to him. If *this man* could be forgiven who had no
chances to make amends for what he had done, how much
more could he receive forgiveness and restoration. He made up
his mind to go home and say to his father, "Father, I have
sinned against heaven and earth and am no longer worthy to be
called your son."

Throughout the service he thought of the things he could
undo and old visions of life and vocation came back to him. It
was not too late. No wonder he sat there silently in the church
until the minister invited him to drop in at the rectory.

The woman who wore mink gave him enough money to go
home. The minister put him in touch with a friend to whom he
could talk in a city near where his family lived. Eric went home.
His father and brother and sister received him with joy. He
went back to college and then into clinical psychology. How
easily he could establish rapport with men and women whom
fate had broken. They kept him looking deep within himself. It
took a long time before he washed out his bitterness and hate,
but with good counseling and effort on his part, he was reborn.
The old darkness and fear would fall on him now and then, but
at such times he would write to the minister at Calvary Church
who would remind him of what happened that Good Friday.

Eric Adams had been defeated by life and by himself and
there seemed little hope for him. Through grace and hard work
he won a victory.

4   Edith Rankin

"Woman, behold your son.
Son, behold your
mother."

In comparison with these other stories, the one of Edith Rankin was not spectacularly tragic, yet its consequences were just as destructive. There are many who may think that life is not as tragic as this cross section indicates. Sitting where I do and seeing into innumerable lives, however, I find that there is hardly a family that does not conceal some great misery, not a life that is well-known that does not bear some literally unbearable agony. We fear that we are alone, and so we hide these burdens. Stop someday on a busy street corner and look at the faces of those who pass by and see how few of them are lightened with any real joy, purpose, or peace. Most people carry a heavy burden. I will never forget the relief when this realization flooded in upon me. Yet only in times of crisis or real fellowship do the masks of men and women crack and slip so that we can see one another as we really are.

Edith Rankin had long lived in the city where Calvary Church stood. There was nothing unusual about her. Her childhood had been without any special incidents, and even the early years of her marriage had been uneventful. She came from the best kind of industrious working parents. Her father had been an energetic laborer and a fixit man in his spare time. She and her brothers and sisters lived in a simple but tidy home in a decent section of town. Her parents had even bought and paid for their own home. About the only remarkable thing about her parents was that, having a difference of view about religion, they decided that their children should select their own. That gave them the freedom to choose none. Edith visited various churches as a child, but she admired her father, and his example of having nothing external to do with religion impressed her greatly. Unconsciously she decided to follow the father's example, as children so often do.

Edith was bright and did well in school. She even went to business school and had a good job before she fell violently in love with her popular handsome husband. At twenty she was married. He was an excellent machinist and made good wages. They soon began a family, and she was far too busy to think of herself; a woman with four small children has to make time to have any private thoughts. As the children grew up, she was busy baking cookies for homeroom parties and served as secretary for the P.T.A.

As the last child neared the end of high school, she noticed that some of her old drive was leaving her. They had been good children and she loved them. She did not understand what was happening to her, and so she closed her eyes to her feelings and forced herself to continue the usual activities. Her home had contained no more religion than that of her parents. Oh, yes, they were very tolerant. The children could go to any church they wished, but if the church asked for any money or suggested commitment, they pulled the children out. They would not stand for any such intolerance, but they were very gracious about it.

The great change came after John, the youngest, left for college. Edith Rankin was fifty-three then. She got up one morning and just did not have the energy to do anything. She did not care. There was no reason for feeling this way as far as she could see, but nothing seemed to matter. She loved her husband in a way, but he was busy in lodge work and spent lots of evenings out with the men. They had grown apart as she had spent more and more time with the children. He was no longer the dapper young man whom she had married, but bald and with a pronounced "bay window." She lay in bed all that day. Her husband came home that evening and asked what was the matter. She said she did not feel well.

After a week or so her husband took her to the family doctor who gave her a lot of tests and found nothing wrong with her. She was in perfect health. Then, she was referred to a psychiatrist who spent half an hour with her. He said she was a manic depressive and prescribed a drug, but it made her no better. When the doctor suggested shock treatments, she refused, for she said to her husband, "Why should I try such a violent and drastic measure when no one has even talked to me. How can these things give me back my meaning." She stopped seeing the doctor.

A year went by in agonized boredom. Now and then she got out of bed and went downtown. Her husband adjusted to the situation tolerantly. He ate out most evenings and moved to one of the rooms that had belonged to the children. Edith talked over her situation with what friends she had, but all they could say was, "Snap out of it. What is the matter with you?" She lay in bed hours on end and read cheap novels or watched television. She no longer combed her hair or cared for her appearance. Her friends became disgusted and deserted her.

So it was on that Good Friday that she wandered, half out of curiosity, half out of despair, into the large church that stood on the corner not far from her house. She loved the chimes that rang from its tower and had been intrigued when they erected the huge cross on the boulevard. She had read a good bit and knew that it was Good Friday. These days some religous knowledge is almost impossible to escape if you read everything that comes your way. Some of her friends said that the minister was a real nice fellow, and one of her children had been rather active at Calvary Church. She was desperate in a quiet way. She was so sick of meaninglessness and its empty misery. She looked at herself and shuddered, but why care?

The minister's meditations were interesting, but it was not the story that affected her as much as the silences between the meditations. there was no television to turn on and no book to pick up. She had to think. How seldom she had done that in the last thirty-odd years—how very seldom. She looked at the other people in the large, impressive church and wondered why they were there. She wondered why they cared, why they were not like her. Like many people she had gone on for years without ever turning in upon herself and asking who she was or what her meaning might be. She avoided silence like the plague.

The picture that touched Edith Rankin the most was the one the minister drew of Jesus' last words to his mother and his friend, "Woman, behold your son" and "Son, behold your mother." Why should he who was dying care about what happened to them after he was gone? She was far from death, and yet she found that she no longer cared anything for anyone. Her children and husband got along without her. What happened to them did not concern her. Even more amazing to her was the response of the woman, Jesus' mother, and the friend. They cared enough for the dying one that they did as he suggested. Instead if giving up everything because her son was dead, instead of abandoning the cause because his master was slain, they went on together. They acted as though there were some meaning in life, as though there were some real, tangible purpose, as if life had a plan, a destiny.

The picture of the woman standing before the cross on which her son died caught hold of Edith Rankin. Here was one, she thought, with real reason to lose heart and hope. She had been accused of fornication or adultery, left with a son when her husband died, seemingly deserted by that son who rose to great renown and acclaim among her people, and now hung there on a cross like a common criminal. Surely Mary had no reason to live, but she possessed some kind of inner certainty. During the silence, Edith meditated on this. She, Edith, had no meaning, no purpose. This was her trouble. Having raised her family she had no function, no value, no meaning or purpose. She was slipping silently and slowly toward death and oblivion. Why should she care? If there were some truth to what this church stood for, to what this woman stood for, to what the son stood for, then there would be a reason to change. She had never before looked this far into her own life.

Out of the depth of her darkness, a light began to burn and a voice spoke, ''Yes, I am here with you, if only you will turn and find me, but I am gracious and I force myself on no one.'' There was a purpose and meaning. It was her task to find it and let it live through her. She heard the rest of the story and the words, ''Father, into your hands. . . .'' She wrestled with something real and powerful, vital and luminous within herself. Something real was there. She wondered whether she could change. She wondered whether anyone would accept her or give her a chance to change. It was just at that moment that the minister came up to her and invited her to stop by. It was all that was needed to start a chain reaction and nudge her will into action.

The rest of the tale is almost trite. It reads like some of the poor novels Edith had read. She went home and ironed her dress and went to the hairdresser. She got out her hat and came back to church on Easter. It was like a new birth for her. She started the confirmation classes which began the day after Easter. She found the minister glad to talk to her, and he gave her books of an amazing kind to read—books that made her soul grow and reach for new goals. She began to help in the church office, joined a church group, and helped put on a dinner at the fair. The women accepted her and made no reference to the past. Instead they praised her apple pie.

Soon she began to share some of what she had found with her children and her husband. He was so impressed by what religion had done for her, that he even came into the church himself. Edith Rankin began to live. She became a person. The rector regularly sent troubled people to her; she would listen to them, give them one of the vacant bedrooms for a day or so and a meal prepared with love. Often this touched people deeply and they changed, too.

Edith's utter lostness and despair were the ground in which the seeds of new life sprouted and grew and bore much fruit. She shared in her master's victory.

5   Norma Carter

"My God, my God,
why have you
forsaken
me?"

Scarcely had Norma Carter begun to speak when she was recognized by the other seven in the rectory living room. This was none other than *the* Norma Carter, so often photographed in screen and video guides. Several of them spoke at once to ask her what on earth had brought her to the rectory that afternoon. She had everything a person could ask for. She had charm, success, a fine family, money, prestige.

How little we know the hearts of those around us; how little we suspect what they endure. She only laughed at those who asked her these questions, and she answered with several questions of her own: "What makes you think I am different from any of the rest of you? Do you think that having outer luxury fills the void of an empty life? Do you have any idea of the will it took me to film that last picture?" She went on to say: "I had come to the conclusion that life held nothing for me, that there was no hope until I listened to that cry of anguish from the cross. I thought that life should be easy, and in externals it was, but there is usually an inner compensation for outer ease. When the blackness of depression struck me, I gave in to it. I did not realize that life takes courage and that no one finds real life without struggle and endurance. I was a coward because life required nothing better of me.

"You all know my history. You probably know it better than I do. My mother was the famous actress and my father a producer. I was brought up on the stage. I had all the right connections. I went from success to success, from triumph to triumph. So many people envy me my husband and well they might, for he is all he is reported to be—kind, considerate, generous. My marriage has been called a model and no woman has three finer children than I have. Why should I be miserable, so much so that only a month ago I tried to take my life, only to find that I was naive about the number of sleeping pills I needed? My husband and the doctor kept it out of the papers.

"There were so few people I could talk to, for one in my position has to be very careful not to gain bad publicity. The depression first came on me about three years ago. It came like a great cloud and enveloped me, paralyzing my will. It was as if a great ball of lead hung from my inner being. I had money, so I canceled my next engagement and went to the Islands for a rest. I soon recovered and began to enjoy life again. Everyone was kind and helpful. I came back to work, but soon the same blackness came over me again. This blackness of spirit was like the pain of an abscess, but the abscess seemed to be on my soul. No one could give me the reason for it, nor a remedy. I tried to talk to my husband, but it only discouraged him and he would shrug his shoulders. I went to talk to a minister who would not even let me finish my tale, but tried to get me to give a benefit for his church. I tried to talk to friends, but they would not believe me.

"I had always attended church and thought myself a good Christian, but I thought of Christianity as a golden rule of right living, of good counsel and self-help directions. I thought of the gospel as sweetness and light. They never made much of the starker side of the message at the popular church that I attended. I did not think of the message of Christ as a vital force to help one in extremity, but as a bit of perfume to add luster to an already full life. I was in agony. No one would take me seriously or had the resources to help me. Even after I tried to take my life, my husband thought it was an accident. Oh, the letdown of writing notes and getting ready to die, only to awaken perfectly well! No one would believe me, and I was thinking seriously of driving the Thunderbird off some cliff as I set out this morning.

"As I passed that cross standing unadorned on the street, I was drawn to it. It was so grim. What a horrible symbol for a happy faith, I thought. I saw people streaming into church. I have never been in Calvary Church, for I seldom came to this part of the city. An unknown force directed the car to the curb and stopped it. I can't say that I did. Mechanically I got out of the car and locked it. I went into the church. I was a little annoyed by the music. It wasn't as good as in the big church that I attend downtown. I was repelled by the story the minister told. It was cruel and barbaric, a story of betrayal, condemnation, injustice. The minister spared none of the gruesome details.

"I almost left, but something kept me there. The story he told, I had to acknowledge to myself, was the Gospel narrative if you really looked at it. I expected the first three words. My minister had spoken a great deal about forgiveness and carrying one's family responsibility. I was not, however, prepared for the impact of the fourth word upon me. It shook me. *Eloi, Eloi, lama sabachthani* . . . my God, my god, why have you forsaken me?. . . It was strange the chord it struck. I had turned away from God because I had thought that the Holy One was interested only in sensible people and in helping those who helped themselves, and here I saw before me a new idea of God, one who cried out in utter desolation and agony, in dereliction and hopelessness. Here was one who could understand me, one who would not shrug his shoulders, one who cared enough to suffer what I was suffering, one who did understand.

"From the pulpit the minister had hung a crucifix—a small wooden one. As I stared at it, the lips seemed to speak to me and say, 'Yes, I know what you bear and if you will walk on, one step at a time, I will guide you through the valley of the shadow of death. I will show you what is wrong and I will bring you to new life, to a new creativity. Trust me and bear on through.' I must confess I was frightened by this experience. I didn't think that God still acted this way, that people had such experiences anymore in these rationalistic days. I thought the age of revelation and miracles was over. But this was the most amazing and solid experience of my life.

"Something happened at that moment. It is hard to say what. There is no new meaning, nor do I yet understand what my problems are, but from that instant I *wanted* to find my way again. I realized that there was a way if I had the courage to keep on it. I sat in the church trying to figure how I could continue on the way which had opened to me. Then the clergyman came up to me and invited me to come over for some tea. I am going to need a lot of help, but at least now I know it's there and I want it. Isn't that half the battle?"

Norma Carter was right. She was going to need a lot of help, but she did receive it. She was wise enough to realize that conversion is only the *first* step in coming to life. So many people think that once they are converted, they are simply to wait for "pie in the sky when they die." The minister referred Miss Carter to a physician of souls who helped her see how she had gone against the very grain of her life, how she had been interested only in herself and her success, how she had forgotten others. The minister helped her to see that God sometimes allows us to come to just such a depression so that we may awaken and come to ourselves and to Life. He showed her that depression, although often an attack of evil that can lead to destruction, is not an entirely evil thing. It can reveal the abscess on our soul that needs treating. The pain is trying to warn us so that our soul will not be destroyed.

She slipped back many times and wondered many times if it was worth the trouble, but she kept at it, sometimes railing at the newfound God. But, strangely, the God she wrestled with and cursed became more real than the one she had believed in formerly. Gradually she came to love this father–mother God and be upheld by the risen One, so much so that her agents were amazed by her new creativity when she returned to work.

Norma Carter found the cure to her emptiness in a real God who demanded of her a different life than she had been leading, a real God who gave her compassion, understanding, rebirth. A God who reached her as he cried, "*Eloi, Eloi, lama sabachthani.*" The comfortable and deadly life of Norma Carter was not beyond the healing power of the wounded one.

Soon she began producing films that gave hope to many people who had lost it. Once a year she invited her seven new friends to her home, and they shared their struggle, growth, and hope. Norma found that she had to share her struggle if she was to stay in touch with the transforming Light and Love.

6   Edna Masters

"I thirst."

It is strange that a cry of pain uttered by a man dying upon a cross could set in motion the healing of a woman who had been crippled by sickness for nearly twelve years, but such is the story of Edna Masters. The minister had heard of her, for she was well-known in the little city where he lived and worked. She was one of those sick people not destroyed by her illness. She remained cheerful and active in spite of her pain and the increasing difficulty she had in getting about. She was admired by her many friends for her grit and determination. She was not defeated by what seemed to be the heavy hand of adversity.

She had every reason to be the fine character she was. Her parents had been active in establishing several of the local agencies in town. Her father had carried on a fine family business in a most exemplary manner. Both her mother and father had been real Christians, who knew their Bible and practiced what they read. When her mother died a few years before, her father built a magnificent chapel in her memory in their church. When he died suddenly, Edna was not surprised to find that all of his affairs were in perfect order. The business was disposed of and his favorite charities were generously aided, while she herself had all she needed to live comfortably. He had planned his affairs so they would be no burden to his ailing daughter.

The only real tragedy in her life had occurred some fifteen years before, and few people knew how deeply she had been hurt. Even her parents never realized just how much the foundations of her life had been shaken. Edna was taught to look for her blessings and to ignore her difficulties, and this she did. She had been very much in love with a young man who had worked for her father, so much in love that she was sure that he was going to marry her and had let her affections carry her beyond her judgment.

The young man was equally in love with her, but he was weak and not faithful. Force of circumstances gave another woman power over him, and so without a word of explanation he dropped Edna and married the other woman. If Edna had any fault, it was that she was too good. Instead of trying to find an explanation, she assumed the fault was hers. She feared telling her father what had happened, partly because of her own guilt, and partly because she did not want to have her erstwhile lover lose his job. Indeed she still loved him and could not bear to have him hurt. Seeing that her heart still went out to Don James and that she must still meet him socially all the time, she drove her feelings deeper and deeper into herself and pretended not to feel at all. It was shortly after this that Edna's health began to break. She had some unexplained fevers and then came the crippling, progressive ailment the doctors could not help in any way. Everyone told her how brave and noble she was to stand up so well under such burdens, and this encouraged her to continue in an attitude of self-sacrificing nobility.

At the time Edna came into the minister's living room she did not realize that this event of so many years ago had played such an important part in her life. She came to the significant realization there that God did not necessarily will her illness and that there might be a way out of it for her.

Two quite different factors brought Edna Masters to Calvary Church on that particular Good Friday. First of all, she didn't like the oratorical contests put on by the local ministerial association in the name of Good Friday. Then, too, she had heard that the new minister at Calvary was sincere and that he held the novel belief that Christian churches should be interested in faith healing—an idea looked upon with scorn by her own church.

She had been in Calvary Church for weddings and funerals while the former rector was there and thought it cold and impersonal. She was impressed, however with this service. The service increased in meaning and power. She saw more and more clearly the awful tragedy of that day, the terrible agony human beings perpetrated on Jesus, the Messiah. Some tragedy is too awful to be understood quickly; one must feel it for a long

time to appreciate its full horror. She had never before sat for
several hours as one man developed one by one the insults,
betrayals, injustices, agonies that Jesus had suffered that day. It
came to her more and more clearly that what Jesus had endured
that day was wrong, utterly wrong, that this was just the polar
opposite of what God intended life to be.

Then she heard the fifth word, as if for the first time, "I
thirst." These words summed up the physical suffering of the
Master. She had never understood why these words had been
the only cry of physical pain from the cross, but now the
preacher explained that he suffered from traumatic thirst—the
thirst of the wounded, thirst caused by a loss of blood. He went
on to tell how people who have been wounded in battle, as well
as those torn apart in accidents, give this cry as the very epitome
of their suffering. She remembered how her father on his
deathbed, when he had so many other things afflicting him,
had begged for water to slake his thirst.

It suddenly struck home to her that just as this pain on the
cross was a terrible thing and against God's will, so was *all
meaningless pain and suffering*. Human agony wasn't just given to
be endured; it was not God's will that she should have suffered
and been crippled as she had been for the last twelve years. This
human being had died upon the cross to reveal the inhumanity
of humans to one another and to show that God could conquer
it. Jesus had tasted the depth of human suffering and despair
and the nadir of human physical suffering in order to conquer it.
It was almost as if she heard these words ringing within her and
gathering other words around them. "I thirsted that you might
not have to suffer, that suffering might be abolished among
broken men and women." The resurrected Jesus was a con-
queror of evil, death, suffering, and pain. He knew the worst
that humans can do to each other and had won a victory.

As she sat there, a host of ideas rushed through her mind.
"Why had she suffered so? What could she do? Where would
she go? How would she start?" She had not even noticed that
everyone else had left, when the minister came up to her and
said, "Won't you stop in for a cup of coffee at the rectory?" She
had almost made up her mind that she would go and see this
minister, and just then he came to her.

She was quiet for a long time before the fire, and then very
tentatively and timidly she offered the idea she had received
from the service, and to her surprise the minister said, "You are

quite correct. God desires the wholeness of every man, woman and child, but sometimes we get in the way and sometimes forces of evil opposed to God's will gain control of us.'' She saw how others had received power and transformation from the service and she felt her pain diminish. She came back again and again to talk with the minister. They soon discovered that she had long ago given up her desire to live, that she had been living a false life out of touch with her feelings, that she had hidden resentments and guilts, that she had really hated herself and others in spite of her mask of nobility and caring.

As she came to herself and sought to be what she was made to be and wrestled with these things conscientiously and honestly, not trying to be something that she ought to be, but rather trying to be herself, Edna Masters slowly recovered her health. She did not leave her former congregation. She took the message of transformation back there in a way that none could ignore or deny. It was a long road, but she made it, for she discovered healing is the first fruit of the victorious resurrected Christ. She visited the sick and was often the instrument of the relief of pain, and the gift of hope and healing.

7   The Reverend Alfred Darby

"It is finished."

The Reverend Alfred Darby had been retired on a disability pension for nearly five years. He was only fifty years old but looked more like sixty-five. His hair was white and there was a tremor in his hand. He was a little more reserved in sharing his own life than the others had been. It is so difficult for clergy because people refuse to recognize they too are human.

Alfred Darby had been looking for help for a long time, but he never found it until this Good Friday. He had been the rector of a very fashionable parish when he broke down the first time seven years before. No one could understand why this happened to Al. He had the best recommendations when he came to St. Athanasius' Parish. He had been associate at one of the foremost churches in the East, and before that had been a curate in a fine New England church. The church had grown and expanded. He had a fine mind, if not a brilliant one. No one could stand against him in a discussion. His sermons were to the point, incisive, thoughtful, and helped many people. The town went wild over him when he first came to his parish. No priest there had ever worked harder or more devotedly. The sick were continually called upon, the factions of the church were healed under his irenic disposition, and former members who had left because an organist had been fired, were won back by his tact and understanding.

After his first year and a half in the parish, some of his more perceptive members noticed that he was more nervous and tense. Then the doctor ordered him to take a six-week rest. He came back full of life, but it quickly left him. He had to take drugs to preach, and then one day in an important meeting he blew up and said things that no one believed him capable of thinking, let alone saying. Again the doctor ordered a rest. Some friends tried to find out what was the matter and help, but it waš no use. He made one more attempt to come back to the parish, and then resigned. He tried other jobs but simply could not handle them. The church retired him on a disability pension, but this wasn't enough for his family to live on, and so his wife and their five children went back to live with her wealthy parents. Alfred tried to live there, but he simply couldn't take their patronizing attitude—they had never approved of the marriage. He left his family and went to Chicago where he took a small room and existed from one day to another.

He tried to go to some lay people for help and their attitude was that, as a priest, he surely should be able to find his own way. In an attempt to get to the bottom of his troubles, he went to some of his clergy friends. However, rather than help, the friends promptly went to the bishop who called him into his office and berated him for his weaknesses. There was nothing to live for, yet he lived on, hardly human.

A former parishioner had asked him to come and spend the Easter vacation with him, and so he came to the little city where Calvary Church was located. He always went to the Good Friday service, although it embarrassed him because people usually asked him who he was and where he was staying, and he had to go through the same sad story once again. He still wore his clerical collar as a symbol of a lost profession.

As he listened to the passion narrative unfold, Alfred Darby was impressed more and more by the courage of the Master. Instead of theological ideas about the Christ, he looked squarely and directly at the human Jesus. The minister said one sentence that struck home to him, "It is our task as Christians to follow God's way for us as Jesus followed God's way for him." This he, Alfred Darby, was not doing. He had not had the courage to stand the turmoils and disputes of his parish, or the courage to face anyone not liking him. He had been afraid to go his own way. What he wanted to do was to have a successful parish and to have everyone admire Alfred Darby—the intellectual, hardworking, consecrated priest.

He never had the courage to find out what his way truly was, the courage to go up to his own holy city, to go through his own Gethsemane, to pass through his own inner crucifixion. He had always tried to protect himself and convince himself that he was of some value, and the only way he knew to do this was to try to get other people to like him. This resulted in frantic efforts that wore him out, made him a physical wreck, and caused him to lose his family, his position and his self-respect.

Alfred Darby thought to himself that if Jesus had been like him, everything would have gone well until the Temple authorities began to cause trouble. As rector, he broke out in a sweat every time the bishop's office called. Had he been in Jesus' place, he would have gone into panic when the crowds began to dwindle! Suddenly he saw his panic for what it had been. It was cowardice—he was running away as fast as he could by standing stock-still. His trouble was acute fear, fear of facing the negatives of life. Strange how much worse our fears usually are than our actual problems. Difficulties cast long shadows. He remembered how in those last days at his parish his heart had begun to beat fast every time the phone rang. He just had not had the courage to bear the tension, and he had broken down.

It was his task to try to follow this man, Jesus, and to try to have courage. It became clear when he heard the words, "It is finished." Jesus had been able to cry these words out upon the cross in the face of every contradiction. He said, "I have completed my task; I have done my work; I have done well and have brought things to perfection." What were the external circumstances? A rejected and deserted prophet dying upon a cross between two criminals. He was so sure of his own way that he could say: "It is finished" (or completed), even under such circumstances. It was then that Alfred Darby received a new impulse to complete his own life, to take it up where he had left if off. Up until that very moment nothing in that Good Friday service had touched him, but now new determination arose within him. He did not know how or where, but he would finish his life, he would complete it, he would bring his life to a satisfactory end. There was a way. He would try again.

He sat long in church wondering how he would begin, and then the rector had come up to him. Something new, something which had been dead for a long time had stirred to life within him, but where he was going he did not know. And so Alfred Darby came to the living room of Calvary rectory. That afternoon he didn't say very much. The rector suggested that he come back the next day. He did, and they talked; he summoned up his courage and told of his inner fears and turmoils and the rector listened, and smiled, and said, "I know what you mean. I have been through such things myself. Only I was fortunate. I found someone to help me through." Thus encouraged, the priest told his whole story. How much they discovered! He had been the pampered only son of middle-class parents who had squandered everything on him. They had tried to make life easy for him, and enabled him to go places where neither of his parents had ever been. Both of them worked so that he could go through college and have the things that only the children of wealthy families had. They did the same when he went to the seminary.

In his teens Alfred had done many things that would have killed his mother had she known of them, for she was always talking about her wonderful son, and about how considerate and thoughtful he was. In order to forget some of his inner feelings and attitudes, which he did not have the courage to bear, he worked harder at school and received the acclaim that his impoverished soul needed in order to survive. He never really thought himself of value, because he was sure that his family would not have accepted him had they known what he had really been and done. Their acceptance seemed to be given only when he lived up to their expectations. When he married, it was to prove to himself that he could and that he was accepted. No wonder the marriage broke up as it did. . . . This story came out over the period of many sessions with the rector.

The rector took him to the bishop, who understood, and then he began to help out in Calvary Church. One by one he faced his fears, faced himself. His courage grew. His way was not an easy one. Many of the people of Calvary parish did not like him, but he continued to do what he saw was right nonetheless. Finally, he invited his family back. This was not easy, either, after four years of separation. Alfred began to follow his way as Christ had followed his own. He found that by going one step at a time, facing each problem honestly as it came, taking the burden of pain and humiliation, gradually restored his courage. His vigor came back, his life, his power, and he began to preach sermons better than he had ever preached before. It was a sad day for Calvary parish when the Rev. Alfred Darby was called to a large and important church in that diocese. The work he did there was the talk of the entire diocese. When he retired many years later, only a few understood the meaning of the words with which he ended his final sermon, "It is finished."

These words had been before him through those years. He had a task to do that no one else could do and it was his job to finish his life. He, like everyone else, had a unique destiny. He must complete it, must bring it to fruition. . . . With Christ's example and help, he did. Victory came after a lifetime of defeat. He kept in touch with those he had met in the rectory living room. They supported him and he supported each of them. How much they needed each other and particularly when each one lost the way. He often told them that they were his real church, what a church ought to be. There can be deep fellowship among those who suffer and are still seeking the light.

8   James Donally

**"Father, into your hands
I commend my
spirit."**

James Donally smiled as he looked around the comfortable rectory living room. He listened intently to what everyone else had said. He had not spoken at all. After the priest had told a bit of his story, there had been a long silence—the kind of silence that speaks of understanding and sharing and not of embarrassment. Then Donally broke the silence and said, "I see that I can trust you. Men and women who know one another on this level can usually trust one another. Do you know what I am, or rather what I have been?" There was a pause, and then he went on. "I have been for fifteen years the tool of the Communist Party. In recent years I have organized wildcat strikes and corrupted your public officials with money which I have received from the party. I organized the unemployed in the depression days and incited riots. I have fermented trouble and strife whenever and wherever the opportunity arose. I work for the KGB."

No one raised an eyebrow. So much had happened that afternoon that nothing seemed impossible. Mr. Donally went on: "I can actually feel a comradeship here in this room that I have been looking for all my life, but it is on a deeper plane than I believed humans capable of. I have seen today, and I have felt today, a depth of my own being and a response from others that I never knew existed.

"Naturally you wonder why I came to your service this afternoon. The reason is very simple. I came from pure curiosity. I had never been to such a service and I came to jeer and laugh. I knew the gospel story and knew that people worshiped this man on a cross, this pale Galilean. I couldn't believe that there could be such a glorification of weakness, and I came to see for myself."

He paused and then went on: "Looking back upon the events of this day, I suppose there were deeper reasons for my coming. I see now that there had long been brewing a secret inner revolt against the beliefs I held. I see that a soul as deep as this one within me cannot be contained forever within the limits of enforced beliefs. Marxists fight a losing battle. You cannot war forever against such power and vitality hidden in the depth of the human soul.

"Do you want to know my story?" He awaited as all assented and then went on. "I'll tell you. I was born forty-five years ago in New York. My parents were emancipated people. They had broken with the church in which they were raised in the old country. They were laboring folk. Both my mother and father worked. There was a large family of us living in two rooms on the lower East Side. My father was a brutal fellow. How my mother lived with him I don't know, but she was no angel, either. When the old man got drunk, he would beat us kids for the slightest breaking of his rules.

"Then I found out one day that my mother was running around on the side. I hated my father and was disgusted with my mother. As soon as I was sure I could make my own way, I left home. I thought I had a sure job, for I was a good worker and the boss liked me, but the company went broke and I was out on the streets at seventeen.

"God, the things I had to put up with in order not to starve. I knew all the bread lines and rescue missions in the city. That's where I first heard the story of Christ. You had to listen to some of their sentimental hymns and a lot of sweetness and light about Jesus before they gave you a lousy bowl of soup. It made me sick, but when you are hungry, you will even put up with creeps like that. The finishing touch was when one of the gospel gals propositioned me. I got out of the place and was complaining loudly down in the park when a fellow came up to me and said, 'We've been watching you and I think you could go for our way.' I was game for anything. They gave me a clean room and some good food and began to tell me their ideas of universal brotherhood and fellowship, of everyone sharing everything they had. Naturally I was sucked in. These fellows made a lot more sense than the people at the rescue mission, and no one else seemed to care. I had been good at school until I quit, and they started me out on my education again. They got me a job.

"Boy, I had to work that next five years. Ten hours during the day at work and then five to six hours in classes, and study every evening—for five years. I knew Karl Marx from cover to cover and Lenin and all their 'theology.' As soon as I was drilled to the satisfaction of the boss, I was given a bunch of fellows to teach. I was really sold. The trouble with you Christians is that you haven't studied your own ideas. You don't even know your bibles. You're lazy. You don't have any guts.

"My first doubts came when we all had to switch our line because Russia made a pact with Nazi Germany. It was easy during the war years when we were fighting together, but after the war it was harder and harder to go the party line. One had to bounce around like a rubber ball. I didn't dare look at my own ideas because I knew my whole life would collapse if I did. I did not have anything else to live by except what those guys gave me those long nights in the cell meetings. So when I couldn't stomach something, I pushed it down and worked all the harder.

"The first thing I knew, I was rising to the top. If you work hard enough, you don't have time to think. I worked sixteen to eighteen hours a day. The real jolt came with the invasion of Hungary and I couldn't entirely forget this, but I worked even harder, and so they picked me to come to your little city here where the party had been able to do so little. It was a tough assignment, but an important one in the overall plan. I had some of the funniest things happen to me when I got here. I began to feel strange fears. I got scared to drive my own car. I couldn't sleep, even when I was so tired I could hardly stand up. My stomach began to give me more and more trouble, and the doctor said that there was nothing that he could do for it.

"This was my condition when I walked into your church a little before noon. I think that I was really looking for something, but I would never have admitted it then. I heard the story told with real dignity, no sentiment, no eyewash, and it suddenly came over me that this fellow, Jesus, had courage. He might have been a fool, but he had courage. I've always admired courage, always. This man walked right into trouble and took the consequences without ever flinching, without ever turning back. One thing they train you to do in the party is to stick by your ideal no matter what the consequences, no matter what they do to you. This man didn't even have the party with him, in fact he was against the party and had the courage to walk calmly into condemnation, abuse, mockery, and physical torture without a word. He wouldn't even take the cup of gall, and he didn't cry out on the cross.

"You know, this Jesus of Nazareth captured my imagination as I listened to the words he spoke. How could anyone have the courage to forgive as he did? And his words of forgiveness have lasted while so many acts and words of hatred and revenge have been swallowed up by history. I nearly wept as he cried out, 'My God, My God, why have you forsaken me?' He had such courage. It didn't seem right to have the end come this way. Here was a real man, no pale Galilean, a real man, strong, powerful, determined, with a purpose of his own. I heard the cry, 'I thirst,' and the cry, 'It is finished,' but they didn't mean much to me. I was still thinking of the horror of it that such a man should have to die like that, pilloried on a cross as a public spectacle.

"And then he cried out, 'Father, into your hands I commend my spirit.' I began to realize that for him even dying on the cross wasn't a final disaster. At the end he had confidence and trust and hope, for he believed that beyond all this misery and inhumanity there was the Father into whose hands he could commend his soul. It was as if I were there personally at the execution and I saw him. I saw the look of peace and victory that came over his face . . . and then it struck home to me. . . . What was the purpose of my life and what I was doing? What did I believe? Would my belief help me in circumstances like his?

"I had been well-trained and might have stood the pain in silence, but there would have been no confidence, no hope, no victory. I realized that even if we gained the whole world and had all people organized in communes, each person having all the necessities of life and time for recreation and art, we still had no meaning to give. Without freedom, and without some purpose to which they could commend their spirit, there would be no point to it all. I began to see how I was going to have to reorganize my whole life. I was a little afraid of what my former friends might do, and I wondered if the Christians would accept me. I was mulling things over when the rector came up and asked me to drop in at his house for a while."

The rest of James Donally's story is rather involved, and this is only a sketch. He broke with the party and went into hiding after his comrades made two attempts on his life. He went to the authorities and made a clean break with his past. Finally, he was given a clean "bill of health." It took a long time and a lot of talking before he got to the bottom of his hostilities—hostilities that went back to his earliest childhood, but gradually he brought the whole of his life into harmony with his new insights. He began to read a lot and talked with the bishop. He was not disillusioned with the failures in the church. He had seen far greater inconsistencies. Eventually, he went into the ministry, for he said, "There is so much to be done. I know how men and women are hungry for meaning. Only one can help, one who knows the hopelessness of people and knows another dimension that can touch them. This man, Jesus, had what it takes. He became what we are in order that we might become what he is. It is never too late. Victory can come out of disaster, cruelty, and even dishonesty."

Donally was one of the first of a great mass of men and women in Eastern Europe and Russia who are looking for more than Marx can give.

Epilogue to Part One

Five years later these eight met at Norma Carter's magnificent home. It was not a solemn gathering. They laughed and joked about their failures and temptations. They had nothing to hide from one another. They shared their successes and joys. These eight knew and cared for each of the others. In their Eucharist, they experienced the one who stood with unhurrying feet among them. The candle that burned there was shining as brightly as a star.

Each of them had found what human beings long for; they had found a fellowship in which they received acceptance and love. The resurrected Jesus was in a real sense with them and had touched each one some 1900 years after his crucifixion. They also saw the risen One in each other. They knew the present reality of the victory. Jesus won on Golgotha over death and evil. They knew that no defeat or lostness, dishonesty or darkness could withstand the light and love of that victory. They also knew that any victories that were not completed in this life would come to fruition in the Kingdom on the other side.

Their fellowship in defeat and victory welded them together into an invisible church. They had found the true church that releases human beings from inner oppression and gives conviction so that outer oppression does not have the last word. Just before they left, Alfred Darby summed up the feelings of the whole group. "How fortunate we are to have found true fellowship. Is not the purpose of the church, the fellowship of the Way, to walk with the defeated so they can find victory and abundant life?"

Then they left one another for another year, certain that they could call on each other at any time. They had experienced a taste of the communion of saints and the land more large than earth, more kind than home. Each of them went a separate and different way bringing to others in defeat the victory that had found them.

Part Two: The Meditations

Responding to the Victory of Jesus' Resurrection

We ask you, life giving and victorious resurrected One, to help us to grasp the full meaning of your victory over suffering, death and evil; and to help us live with hope and love, with joy and expectation, with patience and determination, with confidence and peace as we prepare for transcendent fellowship of eternity that you have opened to us by death and resurrection. May we now know something of the kingdom for which you told us to pray and then know its fullness by growing forever in your loving presence.

Introduction

The resurrection is almost too much for us. How can we assimilate this victory into our daily lives and live within its victory? I offer ten meditations that have been meaningful to me as I have tried to become a resurrection Christian.

It is difficult to deal with anything that we cannot put into images, into story. The Gospel accounts of the resurrection are so different. It was Dorothy Sayers in her book of radio plays, *The Man Born to Be King*, who first opened my understanding to see how these different stories fit together into a single whole. And so we look at the resurrection events as a consecutive narrative. We need to imagine the resurrection before we can meditate upon it.

However, we can keep God out of our lives. The loving Creator has given us the freedom to keep him out. We have the power to reject the Divine Lover as well as to accept the Holy One. How do we open the fortresses of our hearts to God?

The resurrection of Jesus reveals to us the essential nature of the Divine; it is Love. If we are to remain in communion with Love and the resurrected Jesus, we need to be on the narrow, steep path of Love. This essential part of our being has often been crushed by the unloving society in which we have been raised. And, we cannot love anyone to whom we do not listen. Listening is the hallmark of love and Love.

There are times when indignation arises within us as it did in Jesus. Loving does not mean detachment. Sometimes we need to take action where evil is destroying people around us. How can we take that action creatively?

One of the greatest mysteries to those who have experienced something of the love of God is this: ''Why is there evil in God's good world?'' We need to wrestle with this mystery. I find no way to offer a meaningful answer to this enormous problem except through the death and resurrection of Jesus of Nazareth.

Jesus talked about the Kingdom of Heaven and the Kingdom of God all the time. He told us to pray daily for the coming of the Kingdom. He believed that the Kingdom was present in us and among us now but also that we only knew its utter fullness in life after death. Can we still believe in heaven and know what it is like? The conviction that our lives continue after death is a very practical matter. Few human beings can live satisfactorily in the abyss of meaninglessness. Lack of meaning can destroy our bodies as well as our minds and souls. Nothing helps us more in dealing with loss of meaning than Christ's resurrection victory.

The great Christian thinker, Friedrich von Hügel, noted that all of the great saints are characterized by their joy—joy because in the end all will be well. Joy is one of the essential characteristics of living the resurrected life.

The following are meditations. They need to be read meditatively. My suggestion is that they be read one at a time with fifteen to thirty minutes of time for reflection after each one is finished. The reader may wish to read them through and then return to them asking himself: ''How does this apply to me? What more do I need to do to be a better instrument of the risen Jesus?''

Paul makes the following suggestion to the people in Colossae:

> If then you have been raised with Christ, seek the things that are above, where Christ is seated at the right hand of God. Set your minds on things that are above, not on things that are on earth. For you have died, and your life is hid with Christ in God. When Christ who is our life appears, then you also will appear with him in Glory.

Colossians 3:1–4, RSV

1   What Happened at the First Easter?

On the Friday before the Passover in 29 A.D., the occupying army of the Romans crucified three criminals on Golgotha, a hill right outside Jerusalem. The man on the center cross had done no wrong, but he frightened the leaders of the Temple, the religous leaders of the people. Jesus' mother and friends took the body down from the cross and carried the body to the new tomb of Joseph of Arimathea and rolled a great stone in front of the tomb.

The next day was the sabbath and the Jews could do no work, but the women gathered spices needed to embalm Jesus' body. The broken-hearted disciples stayed behind locked doors, frightened, despairing, hopeless. They were afraid the Roman soldiers might come and seize them and crucify them too. Can you imagine how they felt? How deep was their despair! They had not understood Jesus' message of hope—that he would rise again. They thought that his life had come to an end; nothing was left to hope for.

The women, however, were busy making preparations to go early on Sunday morning to the tomb. They would do their last act of loving devotion for their beloved Jesus. As they walked up to the tomb carrying their spices, they wondered how they could move the stone in front of the tomb. As they approached, they were surprised, frightened, and fearful. They saw that the great stone already had been rolled away. They quickened their pace and came to the tomb and looking inside saw an angel in shining, dazzling white clothes. Now they were even more frightened; it is always frightening to behold the Holy, one of God's messengers. The angel told them not to be afraid, that Jesus had risen from the dead and they were to go and tell the disciples and Peter.

The women were terrified and fled. Do you wonder why they fled? Their world was turned upside down. Rome was not the greatest power. A loving God had raised Jesus from the dead. Evil was defeated. Rome was defeated. Eternity had broken in on them. ANYONE WHO IS NOT A LITTLE FRIGHTENED BY THE RESURRECTION, HAS REALLY NOT QUITE UNDERSTOOD IT. God's love and power are real, and we need to live in the Kingdom of God now.

The women told the disciples what they experienced, but no one believed them. However, Peter and John rushed off to the tomb to see for themselves. Peter entered the tomb first and saw the shroud and the napkin that had been around his head lying there as if Jesus' body had just evaporated, but he did not understand. Then John entered and saw that this was not the work of grave robbers. Because he loved so much, he began to understand and he believed that Jesus was now alive. Slowly they walked down the hill and described what they had found to the other disciples, but still they could not believe.

Mary Magdalene had lingered on near the tomb when the other women fled. She was brokenhearted and weeping. Her life had collapsed. She wandered back to the tomb, and even through her tears, she saw the brilliance of two angels within the tomb. They asked her one of the most pathetic questions of all times: "Woman, why are you weeping?" She replied, "They have taken away my Lord and I do not know where they have placed him." And then she caught sight of someone standing behind her. This person again spoke the same words the angels used: "Woman, why are you weeping?" Mary thought that he was a gardener and asked him politely: "Sir, if you have taken him away, tell me where he is and I will take him away." Then Jesus called Mary by name and then she knew it was Jesus and cried, "Rabbouni," and fell at his feet and threw her arms around his legs. Jesus said: "Stop clinging to me, I have not yet ascended to the Father." He raised her to her feet and disappeared from her sight.

Mary was transformed from darkest night to the glory of the brightest day. She skipped and ran down the hill, picking the lilies and throwing them into the air, singing and laughing. JESUS WAS ALIVE. ALL WAS WELL WITH THE WORLD. But the disciples did not believe Mary either.

Why did Jesus appear first to Mary Magdalene? Because she needed him the most. When we are in deep sadness and hopelessness, if we listen, we will hear the Risen Jesus speaking our name and we can be transformed as Mary was and know that all is well.

Two of Jesus' friends were returning home on that same Sunday morning, home to Emmaus. They were talking about the tragic events that had taken place, but they were going back to take up their lives again. A stranger fell into step with them and asked them what they were talking about, and they told him. The stranger began to explain scripture to them, told them how the Messiah had to die and rise again, had to suffer and be raised up. The stranger started to go on, but they asked him to stay with them and so he remained. They brought out food and wine, and the stranger took bread and broke it and their eyes were opened and they knew it was Jesus and he disappeared from their sight.

Why did Jesus appear to these two? Because they kept on going even in their sorrow and pain and they invited Jesus to stay on with them. We too need to keep on going and to invite Jesus into our lives again and again and we, too, may see him in the breaking of the bread.

These two, Cleopas and his friend, looked at one another and the bread broken on the plate and they knew that Jesus was alive, had risen from the dead. They wanted to let the other disciples know about this wonderful news and so they *ran* back the five or six miles to Jerusalem. They pounded on the door where the disciples were hidden and finally the door was opened to them and they blurted out their news: "Jesus is risen. He is risen indeed." The disciples were ecstatic; they told the same story: "The Lord has been raised. It is true. He has appeared to Simon."

While they were still speaking, Jesus appeared in their midst and said: "Peace be with you." Again the disciples were frightened and acted as though they were seeing a ghost. And Jesus asked them: "Why are you so upset. Can't you see that it is I? Look at my wounded hands and feet and see that it is truly me, flesh and blood." Then he shared a meal with them; he asked them for some food to eat. Why is it so hard for us to believe that Jesus could appear both in a vision and in solid reality? The God who created this incredibly complex and mysterious universe can raise Jesus in many different ways for us.

These disciples had a big job ahead of them. They found that

God was love and that he had conquered evil and came even to those who had fled in terror from him when the temple police came to take him in the garden. The same risen Jesus still comes knocking at the doorways of our souls, to us who are no more faithful than those disciples. What incredible and wonderful Love.

The disciple Thomas was not with the disciples when Jesus had appeared to them. He could not believe that Jesus was really raised and said to his friends: "I will never believe Jesus' resurrection until I can put my fingers into the wounds of his hands and feet and my hand into his side." A week later Thomas was with the disciples and Jesus appeared to them all and greeted them: "Peace be with you." Then turning to Thomas he said: "Take your finger and examine my hands. Put your hand into my side. Don't persist in your unbelief, but believe." Thomas fell to his knees and exclaimed in wonder: "My Lord and my God." Jesus loved the doubter as well as the others because Thomas kept on seeking and hoping. Jesus came with tender love and compassion to Thomas and removed his doubt. Then he said to Thomas: "You became a believer because you saw me. Blessed are they who have not seen me and have believed." Blessed are they indeed.

Still the disciples did not get the full meaning of how the resurrection of Jesus should change their lives. One day Peter invited the disciples to go fishing on the sea of Galilee. They went out at night and toiled all night long and didn't catch a single fish. As dawn was breaking, they saw a man standing on the beach. He called out to them: "Young men, have you caught anything to eat?" They called back: "Not a thing." The man told them to cast their net on the other side of the ship, and when they did, they enclosed so many fish that they could not draw the net into the boat. John then realized that it was Jesus and told Peter that it was the Lord. Peter remembered the first catch of fish after Jesus had called him. He was so excited he jumped into the water and waded to the shore. There stood Jesus beside a fire with some bread on it. When the others came, Jesus told them to bring some of the fish that they had just caught and he placed them on the fire. Then Jesus told them to come and have their breakfast. They knew it was Jesus, but they were afraid to ask him. There was something unearthly about him. But they came over and Jesus fed them with the bread and the fish, and then they began to speak more comfortably with him.

When the meal was over, Jesus took Peter aside and asked him three times if he loved him. He asked three times to undo Peter's three denials. He loved this man who had denied him so much that he wanted to free him of guilt. Then he gave Peter three different commands: "Feed my lambs. Tend my sheep. Feed my sheep." DOES NOT JESUS SPEAK TO US WHEN WE ARE QUIET ASKING US IF WE LOVE HIM AND THEN TELLING US TO TAKE CARE OF HIS LAMBS AND HIS SHEEP? Jesus then predicted Peter's martyrdom and Peter saw John nearby and said: "What about him?" And Jesus replied that this was not Peter's concern and then said to Peter: "Your business is to follow me." Is this not our task too? Not to worry about other people but to follow him ourselves as best we can.

Jesus appeared one more time to his disciples and then disappeared from them in a blaze of glory. By this time the disciples realized that Jesus was not leaving them, but rather returning to the Father to be always and everywhere available to them. It was this cosmic return that made Jesus infinitely available to all of us always. The disciples then returned to Jerusalem with great joy to await the giving of the Holy Spirit on Pentecost. As we meditate on this event, we know that Jesus has risen from the dead and is with us always. There is nothing left to fear. All is well.

The hymn we quoted in part in the introduction to this book I now quote in full. Few modern words provide a better subject for our meditations on resurrection life.

> And have the bright immensities
>   Received our risen Lord,
> Where light years frame the Pleiedes
>   And point Orion's sword?
> Do flaming suns his footsteps trace
>   Through corridors sublime,
> The Lord of interstellar space
>   And Conqueror of time?
>
> The heaven that hides him from our sight
>   Knows neither near or far
> An altar candle sheds its light
>   As surely as a star,
> And where his loving people meet
>   To share the gift divine
> There stands he with unhurrying feet;
>   There heavenly splendors shine.

As we step into the Easter mystery, may we also know that the risen loving Jesus is always at our side and that we meet him in the gathering of his friends each Sunday, the weekly celebration of Easter. And may we know that in the end all will be well.

2   Letting God In

There is something more powerful than God. It is the human race. Yes, we are more powerful than God in a most important way. You and I can keep God out of our lives, not only here and now, but forever.

God is gracious. He has set a limit for Divine Power and will never step beyond it. The Holy never breaks into a human life and remains there unless Love is desired, unless the door is opened and God is invited in.

That is how we become more powerful than God. The inner fortress of our soul is ours, and not even God will break into it unless we want God and open the door and welcome Love. Any of us can keep our lives closed to God forever.

God stands outside the human soul, ready to come in. The best representation of this is the famous picture, "The Light of the World," which shows Christ standing at a doorway that has no latch on the outside. There the risen Jesus stands, lantern in hand, knocking. Thus does God come to us, waiting, eager to enter, but never stepping over the threshold until we open from the inside.

Love Must be Free

Why does not God just knock down the door and come in? Why does the Holy stand waiting? Why does God give us the freedom to reject and turn God down? Why? Because God wants to have a relationship with us, not a forced one and does not want to relate to us as slaves. This would be no real relationship: there would be no possibility of love under these circumstances. You cannot love unless you have the right and power to reject love. You cannot form a true relationship unless you are free not to relate.

Love and relationship must be free actions or they cannot exit. For some mysterious reason beyond my comprehension, God want us to love him. Indeed, Divine Love created us so that there might be the reality we call love, so that God might have someone to love him and to be loved by. To make it possible, God has taken the great risk, the incredible chance of creating something in the universe that could resist Love and even pretend that the Divine does not exist. Only thus could we have the freedom to genuinely love God.

Real religion begins when suddenly we awaken to the marvelous mercy and goodness of God and begin to love the Holy out of pure affection and desire. To achieve it, God dares to give us power to reject and ignore the Divine, shut our lives tight against Divine Love.

God's Overtures

God has so made us that we can never have any satisfaction with life, any abiding fulfillment without God. But the Holy One gives us the freedom to find this out for ourselves and not force this fact upon us. Still we have been given many hints of Divine Love. God has broken through to us in the great religions of humankind and in the revelations to Moses and the prophets. Then the Divine came among us in Jesus of Nazareth who died and rose again to express love at the heart of Being. Sometimes the Holy Spirit troubles our sleep when we are on the wrong path and at other times gives us dreams and visions. The spirit of God performs signs and wonders for us, but never forces us to believe or accept the offered hand of Love. Acceptance of Love is our own free action. If we prefer to remain separated from the Divine, if we wish to try to remain satisfied with our own petty human goals, with our own egos, then we may do so. We can remain within the narrow life of our own petty egotism hungering for something more, we know not what. But God still stands outside knocking on the well-locked doors of our souls.

Hell is simply the reality of keeping God forever out of our lives. Hell is nothing more than remaining eternally within the boundaries of our own egos, when there is a deep thirst in us for something more. Hell is trying to find life where there is no life to be found. Hell is drilling eternally for water, where there is no water. Hell is not a punishment, but rather the simple result of rejecting the reality and love of God. It is seeking darkness rather than light, when the depth of our being yearns for light and will not admit it. On the other hand, heaven is simply being fulfilled in the presence of God, having Divine Love forever.

Two Worlds

Many of us seem to be afraid that God is dead. What people are really saying is that they are afraid that God, as a reality to which we can relate, has never lived. When we try to find God only in the world of space and time, only out there in space, only in the material world, we will naturally come to this conclusion. If we look for God as we look for an atom or a star or a human being, then we will never find any God at all. This is why the Hebrews were so dead set against idolatry, against tying God down to one place or time. God is not going to be found in one particular image or place.

As long as we think that there is only one world, a material world, and that there is no other world, God will appear dead—we won't be able to find Divine Love. We have to realize that there is another world, a spiritual, non-physical or psychic world (call it whatever you please)—a realm of reality other than the physical and material one. We can touch this world through our inner experiences and through our dreams and strange intimations, in our sharing in other lives.

The spiritual world is real. We find it in the reality of our own psychic life, of our own consciousness. It is closer to us than even the material world, so close to us that we do not even see that it is there. We can learn to know this reality better and deeper, however; and as we do, we find the reality of the God who has created not only the physical, material world, but the spiritual one as well. This is not fancy but reality. It is true.

How can we know that this is true? By using the method that reveals this inner spiritual world and the God who dwells transcendently and immanently in it. If we refuse to use the method that has been provided by every important religion from the beginning of time, we will not discover this world. It is like denying the existence of Jupiter's moons and refusing to use a telescope to verify your opinion. I do not have much patience with this kind of disbelief.

Encountering God

The method that I am referring to is nearly as sure as that of the telescope, but it is an inner method because you are looking for an inner spiritual reality. What is this method? It has five parts. This is the way we can let God into our lives and get to know the Holy One:

1. First of all we must give the idea that there is a spiritual world and a reality such as God the chance of being a possibility. We must pose the hypothesis and then try it out. God will never break into our lives unless we turn toward him and entertain Divine Reality as a possibility.

2. There must also be times of quiet and silence in which we can turn away from the outer world, away from complete absorption in the physical world, in doing and busyness. In quiet we can come to an inner honesty and self-confrontation and a facing of ultimate issues and realities. Without silence there can be no inner life, and the reality of God and the spiritual world can never, never, never be known.

3. Then we must develop another kind of thinking than the one we use most of the time, a kind of thinking that springs from the depth of our being—imagination. We have more faculties in our human psyche than we ordinarily realize. Imagination shows itself in art and literature, in mythology and creativity. Although it must be disciplined by reason, imagination takes us to places where reason could never climb. The reality of what this imaginative thinking brings us can be tested and verified. We must learn to use the soul's imagination.

4. We must listen to the strange intimations that break in upon us, our dreams, our visionary experiences. We must take seriously our experiences that carry us beyond the limits of our egos. We can laugh at them and ignore them; but if we will look and listen to them, we shall find the reality of the spiritual world very close. Those who want a nonreligious verification of this truth should read Jung's *Memories, Dreams and Reflections* in which the greatest psychiatrist of our time has described the experiences that occurred in his life. Then they can go back and look seriously at the wonders in the New Testament and see how God and the spiritual world have tried to present themselves for consideration.

5. The fifth suggestion is that we live the way of charity and concern for others. Those who are not generous of their material goods and do not try to love those around them, turn themselves away from God and can never find or be found by the Holy One. This is the simple truth.

There is no great mystery as to the way in which we open the door to the God who waits outside the human soul desiring to enter and relate. The way that I have described opens our life so that the gracious and loving God who dwells in the heaven, which lies about us, can come in and relate to us and give us the fulfillment that we seek. We pray, "Our Father, who art in heaven. . . . ." Our Father dwells in the heaven which lies inside us, in the heaven with which we have direct contact. There stands the God who is, waiting. . . .

Remember that being *found* of God is not inevitable. We can avoid God if we wish to go our own ordinary way. We can keep God out of our life because in this one way we are more powerful than God.

God has loved us so much that Divine Love has given us this much power.

So much has the real God loved us.

3   Listening

The fine art of listening will unlock more doors into life than anything else I can think of.

"Listening?" you say incredulously. "And what good can it do to learn how to listen?" The answer may sound presumptuous, but it is the truth. First of all, listening is vital because we can love only those human beings to whom we listen—and love is the heart of the spiritual way. The second reason is even more startling: No one can ever learn to listen to God or to the spiritual who has not first learned to listen to human beings! The one who cannot listen cannot love either another or God!

If listening is as important as all this, I'm sure you'll agree with me that it is certainly time that we learn what it is and how to do it.

What Is Listening?

Listening is *being silent with another person in an active way*. It is silently bearing with another person. Some people are silent, but they are not open and active. They are either asleep or dead within themselves. The true listener is one who is quiet and yet sensitive toward another person, open and active, receptive and alive. Listening is participating in another life in the most creative and powerful way. It is neither coercive nor forcing. Rather, it is bearing one another's burdens.

Obviously, we cannot listen until we cease talking ourselves. And it is hard for most of us human beings to halt our chatter. No member of our body is more difficult to control than the tongue. It seems at times to have a life of its own, a life quite independent of us and our rational control.

Too much chatter is usually a form of shyness. We are too insecure to be silent. A wall of words keeps us insulated from others. If we talk enough, we can prevent people from touching us and avoid real communion with others. Continuous talk achieves the same result as social isolation: it obstructs real contact with other human beings and therefore with life itself. This is the supreme form of cowardice and can lead to serious spiritual and psychological difficulties.

Being Silent with Others

The first step in listening, then, is allowing oneself to be with other people and to be silent with them. We are silent not only with our lips but also in our inner response. We listen to them and are silent inside. We neither agree nor disagree with what is said. We simply listen openly, permitting the other person to be what he or she is, and that freely. Listening is free and open and does not need to control what is heard, does not need to censor it.

Those who can listen are secure within themselves. They know where they stand and what they believe. They are not easily upset or shocked. Some people cannot read books with which they do not agree. They must fight with the author and so can get little value from what is written. The same kind of person finds it difficult to listen to another who has different ideas or who has done things of which he or she disapproves. This kind of person is not secure enough in his/her beliefs. They fear that the ground may be swept out from under their feet and so they dare not listen without reactions, emotional and verbal, without vociferous dissent—as if opinion expressed with emotion were a protection. One must develop an inner security in order to listen deeply.

The Listener Benefits

There is another strange truth about listening. The people who learn to listen also strengthen their own convictions and broaden the base of their faith. By a deep and mysterious chemistry of the spirit, the listener is established in life and given roots that reach down into the heart of things. Real listening establishes faith and confidence. It begins by an act of will and ends by reinforcing the will that began it.

Those who listen creatively, however, do not remain always silent. Instead they reflect with the other person, to use the term of Carl Rogers. They amplify and clarify what the speaker says. They may ask for more detail, but always with the intention of finding out what is in the other person and bearing it with him or her. Listening is never artificial or stilted. It is warm, interested, concerned. It seeks to know and to care. Listening is love in action.

On another level, real listening is a kind of prayer, for as we listen, we penetrate through the human ego and hear the Spirit of God, which dwells in the heart of everyone. Real listening is a religious experience. Often, when I have listened deeply to another, I have the same sense of awe as when I am alone in the church at night. I have entered into a holy place and communed with the heart of being itself.

Bearing with the Beginnings

We never find this level in another human being until we first are able to listen to the more superficial levels of that person. We must be willing to hear about all the petty concerns and interests and desires and hopes. We must listen to descriptions of events that have been meaningful and sad to that person. As we do this, we bear with another human ego in its littleness and pettiness, with its frustrations and hopes.

If we can learn to do this, then as we listen carefully and watch, we shall hear that person make a tentative statement of something more. It comes very slowly and gently. We shall find that the other is trying to let us into a deeper and more sensitive level of his/her being. The novel experience of being listened to has raised hope. Perhaps there is another who cares after all— one who would understand! Certainly we can never believe that a person cares about us until he will listen to us.

If we accept these first tentative tests of our acceptance, then the floodgates open and all of us pours out—our entire being with our guilts and faults and sins, with our sense of despair and inadequacy and loneliness, with our self-hatred and self-judgment and inner psychic pain.

This is hard to bear, for all of us have these dark areas of our souls; and to hear another's stirs up our own pain and loneliness. One man, whose business it is to listen to others, found it necessary to go away for a month now and then to discharge the poison that he had picked up in listening.

Yet if we do not listen to the dark side of other persons, we never see them in depth. They remain for us like a child's painting, with no shadow or perspective. A friend of mine, who had revealed to me the worst about himself, decided henceforth to carry his burdens by himself. He might just as well have stayed away, since I no longer knew him. Finally he realized it and wrote me, saying that we can only know others as we know their darkness as well as their light.

Temple of the Soul

When we listen on this level, we begin to hear strange echoes, to see lights and catch the strains of a mysterious music of the soul. When we can accept the darkness and ugliness in another, we see beyond it a beauty that we never dreamed existed. We then touch the deepest levels of the incredible human psyche where dwells the spirit of the living Christ, the Holy Spirit, a reality of the greatest power and love and beauty who will guide us into the deepest reaches of the spiritual world. Indeed, as we listen to another and listen with courage to the demonic darkness that is found in all of us, then suddenly the veil lifts and we find that within another human being we have communion with God, the Holy One.

It makes no difference how depraved or how simple the person is, there is the central fortress of the soul wherein dwells God. This is why all of us are so valuable, so incalculably valuable that no one may ever be used as a means, but only as an end. There is something divine in every human being, and in listening fully we come to communion with it.

As we learn to listen to people and find this element in them, we come to love them with divine charity, because they are God-bearers. We are awed, utterly awed, by the mystery and depth of the human soul that carries within it a spirit such as this. Indeed, I doubt if anyone ever really penetrates into the deepest recesses of another soul who does not arrive at this awe. Something instinctive in us keeps this level closed except for those who develop this kind of reverence, those who can listen in holy awe. Obviously, when we have this kind of reverence for others, we do not repeat what they have told us. What we have heard becomes our holy secret.

Worth Beyond Words

The value of this kind of listening is beyond words. All human relationships are based upon it. Indeed, human communication and fellowship is literally impossible without it. How can we love and deal creatively with a person we do not know? How can we know someone to whom we have not listened? The ability to listen is a prerequisite to love. All creative human relationship is based upon listening.

Unless we listen to human beings, we do not know what they are. So we treat them as what we think they are, rather than what they really are. In such cases, we project either positive or negative elements of ourselves upon other human beings and try to force them into the pattern of what we think they ought to be. This may be a kind of communication with ourselves, but it is certainly no communication with the other person and no basis for real relationship.

To Whom?

And to whom should we listen? To our children? How else can we get to know what they are and help them become what they are capable of becoming? To our husband or wife? To our neighbors? Friends? Enemies? Employer? Employees? To the clerk in the store, the one who delivers water/the paper, the stranger? How else can we come to know the human beings in our life and permit love to begin to move within us?

In addition to all this, there is no other way to learn to listen to God except by learning to listen to human beings. Listening can become a way of life, a habit, and then it opens up not only human relationships but the whole realm of the spirit as well. Our soul develops a new faculty and turns it to a new reality. We realize that the Spirit of God, which we have found in the human soul, can be met and listened to directly, too.

But the Lord is in his holy temple;
  let all the earth keep silence before him.

—Habakkuk 2:20

Be still, and know that I am God.

—Psalm 46:10

4   Patience and Knowing God

As the delightful old saying goes, patience and perseverance made a bishop of his reverence. However that may be, it is certainly true that nobody ever develops religiously without patience.

Yet we encounter a strange attitude in our churches. Religion is something people expect to get in six easy lessons. They think they are going to know all about God in six months.

Patience and Human Knowledge

For this mentality to exist in the modern world is astonishing. Look at the time it takes to become a doctor or an atomic physicist, a lawyer or a college professor. First of all, there are twelve years of basic training in elementary and high school. Then follow four years of college and three or four more of graduate study. Even after all that, who would go to a lawyer fresh out of the university with an important case? Or, who would pick a doctor who just finished internship for a life-and-death operation? We all demand another four to six years of experience before we think of a professional as an expert.

How small we make our God. We think of the Holy One unconsciously—even if we have put away such ideas consciously—as a kind of wooden monarch high in the heavens. We don't even treat God with the respect that we give another human being. What human being have you ever known well in six months? I have been married forty-eight years, yet I am constantly finding out wonderful new things about my wife. I have known my grown-up children since their birth, but I am always discovering new elements and depth within them. In my many counseling sessions, individuals try their best to let me know them. I am simply astounded at the new levels of their beings, the surprising profundity of their personalities. I have never known a human being well before for whom I have not felt awe as of a vast unknown just beginning to open up in front of me.

And we think we can learn to know God in an hour on Sunday morning or in a book or two? If God is God at all, the Holy One is the deepest and richest, the most marvelous and diverse, the most complex and boundless reality that exists. How could we pretend to be more than novices, even after years of devoted study? Yet, whatever their ignorance in other things, every man and woman has opinions about God. And what is worse, they often pay no attention to those who have lived and studied and confronted God for years.

Lessons from the Early Church

The church is largely responsible for this sorry state of affairs. It assumes that we are all brought up in a Christian civilization, and therefore all a person needs do to join a church is come to a few lectures—or maybe none at all.

The Christians of the first centuries would turn over in their graves at the thought of such a procedure. For the first three hundred years of the church's life, those who wanted to be counted among the Christians had to attend three years of classes and be tested in a multitude of ways before they were allowed to be baptized. They knew their faith. They knew their bibles. They knew God. The church of those times was alive, precisely because it was a society of people who knew God. And for that reason it also had power, unbelievable power, a power that outfought and outlived the ancient world.

Unlearning Materialism

We suppose that we live in a Christian society. How we fool ourselves. We live in a world that gives little value to spiritual things unless they produce material results. It is the dollar that most colors our thinking, the dollar with its material power. If we suggest the Christian way on Wall Street or Madison Avenue, we are told to be realistic: this way doesn't work in our world. How deeply this materialism has crept into our thinking: the material is real and only the material. . . . How much like the basic thinking of Marx this is, how similar to his philosophy of dialectical materialism—a philosophy that has not worked.

Yes, we all admit that such a prolonged period of training and practice is absolutely necessary before a person can become proficient in one tiny area of *human* knowledge—the atom, the human body or a part of it, law or some specialized field within it. And yet we expect to know overnight the God, who, if there is one, is the source and ground of all these things and everything else besides.

Patience and Knowledge of God

More than for any other reason, people fail to mature religiously because they don't have the patience to learn and grow. Yet there simply is no short cut to real religion and a vital knowledge of God. Those who would know God well must turn again and again and again, receive fresh insights, assimilate new understanding. We deal with an inexhaustible reality when we deal with God. There is no limit to the depths we may plumb or the facets we may discover or the new aspects of relationship that are ours in coming to God. Indeed, a God who can be easily understood and encompassed isn't worth worshipping.

This is the world in which we are raised. If we would believe in a real spiritual God, in a world of spiritual reality, how much we must *unlearn* before we can learn anything at all. It takes time, patience, perseverance, endurance and the conviction that there is something of value to learn here.

No Plateaus

For this reason, the cult of youth in churches today distresses me. Find a young minister who can interest all the young people and get them enthused. Get things moving! This may make strong institutions, but it has nothing to do with religion, with knowing and loving God and making this reality the center and focus of our lives.

Knowledge of God usually comes slowly. I have been learning about God for fifty-two years, and I shudder to recall the first fourteen of them. Each year I think I have arrived at some kind of plateau, and then I find such marvelous new things that I am amazed that I was satisfied where I was.

No one achieves a vital relationship with God in a short time. But the surprising thing is that those who have kept at it over the years all testify to finding the same divine nature. They are not manufacturing their own ideas; they are discovering the most valuable reality in the world—the core of meaning that makes life worthwhile.

St. Paul, after his conversion experience on the Damascus road, went into seclusion for many years until he had worked out the implications of his faith clearly enough to expound them to others—many years of growth. It took Brother Lawrence ten to fifteen years to achieve his towering stature. Thomas Kelly's magnificent insight came only after twenty years of growth and development. I could go on and on—Augustine, Francis, William Law, John Bunyan, Wesley, Phillips Brooks, the author of the *Imitation of Christ*, Douglas Steere. . . .

Persevering to Maturity

There are no child prodigies religiously, because one of the main ingredients of real religion, one of the things that God demands of humans is patience, grit, perseverance, stick-to-itiveness, endurance. God is a wise parent who wants mature sons and daughters for spiritual children. God knows that unless we develop patience, unless we keep at our religious life, we do not become what we can become. And unless we grow, God's heaven's cannot reveal his most treasured insights and glorious gifts to us.

No one achieves any significant spiritual stature in just a few years of striving. Religion that comes quickly goes quickly. Nothing takes the place of slow, steady growth in coming to know God and being enlightened by the Spirit.

How much do you want to have real meaning for your life?
How much do you want to have your life unified and whole?
How much do you want a transcendental center for your life?

If you desire these things very much and have patience—
plodding, unrelenting patience, you can have them.

It is patience that makes a whole person from the fragmented
parts.

It is patience that makes a mature person of the neurotic.

It is patience that makes a saint of the ordinary person.

Those who seek God consistently, faithfully, determinedly,
doggedly, will not be disappointed. They will find God—and all
good things besides.

5 Righting Wrongs with Christ

How seldom do we see the actual figure of Jesus as he walks through the pages of the New Testament.

Most of the time, unless we stop and listen very carefully, we notice only what we want to, rather than what is there. We humans are experts in avoiding what is unpleasant and uncomfortable.

Thus the average Christian church and the average Christian see a Christ who is anything but the real person in the gospels. We picture a man of sweetness and light, ever gentle and kindly, thoughtful and self-effacing. He almost takes on the air of a beneficent uncle.

We fail to observe the dimensions of power and vigor, of decisiveness and firmness—almost sharpness. We overlook the facts that he spent more time healing the sick than he did in preaching, more time in company that we would spurn than in socially acceptable circles. The real Christ was a person of such tremendous strength and vitality that some people called him the Son of God.

In loyalty to the risen Jesus, his disciples had the courage to go forth and outlive, outfight and outdie the ancient world. This would have been impossible unless the pre-resurrected Christ was of towering stature. Jesus of Nazareth made such an impact that ordinary people like you and me were able to launch a church that has conquered every empire and come through innumerable vicissitudes.

The Angry Christ

A story in the first chapter of St. Mark's gospel depicts the real Christ in a striking way, especially as the *New English Bible* translates it.

It is the story of the leper who kneels before Jesus and says, "If only you will, you can cleanse me." The *New English Bible* gives Jesus' reply in these words: "In warm indignation Jesus stretched out his hand, touched him, and said, 'Indeed I will; be clean again.' " The leprosy disappeared immediately. Then Jesus sent the man away with a "stern warning" not to tell anyone about it except the priest who, according to the law of Moses, had to certify the cure. The man instead spread the news far and wide.

If we will listen to this story, we will get quite a different picture of the Christ than the traditional one. Here was the Son of Man in an angry mood. The Greek original indicates clearly that he was stirred up and angry. Not at all impassive and detached, Jesus became involved deeply and personally in life. *Jesus cared and let his concern show in a very dramatic and personal way.*

Here is one of the basic differences between Christianity and most of the religions of the East. Most Oriental religions tell us that we should not get too involved, that we should have a pious, detached point of view so that nothing disturbs us. Nothing could be further from the life and action of Jesus.

The Involved Christ

He became so involved with life that he took up a whip and drove the buyers and sellers and their cattle out of the temple. He was so incensed at the hypocrisy of the scribes and pharisees that he denounced them in language that ensured his death. Jesus was so upset with people who wouldn't make a decision between the way of life and the way of death that he declared in no uncertain terms that those who go the broad way come to destruction; those who refuse to follow their best light and prepare for the life to come will find weeping and gnashing of teeth as their reward.

Jesus' concern is the key to the understanding of his encounter with the leper. When the sick man asked to be healed, Jesus was first warmly indignant and then gave the man a stern warning. Why? Why was Jesus stirred up and angry?

Foe of All Evil

In the first place, Jesus was always a little belligerent in the presence of sickness. As the incarnation of creativity and life and health, he was unalterably opposed to illness and disease. These things were the work of evil in the universe, and Christ was against evil in all of its forms—*all* of them. He warred against evil. He hated leprosy.

In fact, "The Son of God appeared for this very reason, to destroy the Devil's works" (I John 3:8 TEV). Jesus came to rout evil in all its manifestations. No wonder he became angry when the leper implied that he might not be the enemy of sickness, the evil that attacks our bodies.

In the second place, Jesus was angry because the leper doubted his desire to help him. He looked at Jesus and said in effect, "If you want to help, you can; but you probably don't want to." The man distrusted Jesus' good will, his concern for human beings, his desire to do the right thing. Few reactions cut us more painfully than that! Jesus was truly human. He felt the way we all do when our good will is brought into question.

Harnessing Indignation

Under such circumstances, I think there is a place for some warmth of feeling, some honest indignation—even among Christians—and even though it leads to friction and difficulty. Jesus never said that we should have no negative feelings or conflicts, only that these should never remain unresolved or bandied about behind another's back. We can reconcile only the conflicts that we face.

Christ's indignation, however, did not keep him from healing the leper. Perhaps the very intensity of his feeling aided the cure. There is a wonderful story of an early Christian saint who anointed a man's throat to cure a growth, but it did not go away. He anointed the man a second and third time with no better result. Then, in anger, he forced the whole vial of holy oil down the person's throat, and the growth disappeared.

There is nothing wrong with indignation as long as there is still a basic desire to help and not to hinder, as long as good will persists. Indeed, the indignation may even supply some motive power to good will. The person who cannot feel some indignation and anger probably cannot feel love either. The two are intimately related.

Paul says as much in his letter to the Ephesians: "If you are angry, let it be without sin. The sun must not go down on your wrath; do not give the devil a chance to work on you" (4:26–27 NAB). He does not command us never to get angry, but to make sure our anger does not arise from wounded pride or bad temper, to avoid losing our good will toward others.

Even though Jesus was displeased with the leper, he still cured him. "Then he dismissed him with this stern warning: 'Be sure you say nothing to anybody' " (Mark 1:43–44 NAB). Being the kind of man he was, the ex-leper disobeyed Jesus and told the story to everyone he met, with the result that Jesus was besieged by crowds and no longer had a spare moment to himself.

I think Jesus knew that this would happen. But it is almost as if he couldn't stop himself: when he came face to face with evil—even in such a man—he couldn't help but reach out and defeat the evil. It was his nature to hate evil in all its forms and make war against it.

As Master, So Disciple

The notion that we Christians should merely be passive and look with detachment upon the world, that we should pay attention only to our own souls, is an utter perversion of Jesus and Christianity. The fasting and prayer that does not lead into some form of positive and definitive action simply hasn't caught the idea of Jesus, who was warmly indignant about every kind of evil and stretched out his hand to heal and restore and make new.

Few of us may have the power to heal with a word as Jesus did, but each of us can do something to add to the balance of creativity and hope and happiness in the world. If some evil in the world doesn't make us angry enough to fight it, then I wonder if we are really followers of Jesus Christ. True disciples resemble their master.

What can we do?

We can all get tough with ourselves and begin uprooting those vices we have grown so fond of.

We can be homemakers stamping out gossip and backbiting because they make us burn with indignation.

We can be workers who battle featherbedding and wasted time because they gall our Christian conscience.

We can be young people who resist peer pressure to drink, to take drugs.

We can be businessmen and politicians contending against dishonesty and corruption because these evils enrage us.

We can be nurses, teachers, and social workers who treat people as individual persons and not as numbers and cases.

We can be lawyers fighting for better laws because we hate injustice and doctors combating sickness because suffering makes us indignant.

We can be managers and administrators who won't stand for abuse of power and position.

Look around you. Look at your own home, your neighborhood, your school, your church, your city, state and federal government. What evil makes you angry? What is the wrong you complain about but never do the least thing to set right? In prayer see what the Holy Spirit wants you to do about it.

Our light, the light of Christ in us, must shine before the world. Only then will men and women everywhere see that God is their ally against every form of evil. Only then will they believe that Jesus offers the fullness of life.

6   Why Evil in God's World?

In the gospel of Mark, just as Jesus set his face toward Jerusalem for the last time, we find these remarkable words: "And they were on the road, going up to Jerusalem, and Jesus was walking ahead of them; and they were amazed, and those who followed were afraid. And taking the twelve again, he began to tell them what was to happen to him. . . ." (Mark 10:32 RSV).

Even before Jesus told them of the dreadful events that were to follow them—the betrayal and mocking and crucifixion— even before this, something about him sent chills up and down their spines. Something had happened. There was something so different, so holy, so God-like about Jesus that they were awe-struck. In terror they followed him.

What was it that the disciples sensed in this unique moment? Up to this time Jesus' ministry had been a pastoral one. They had been with him as he traveled up and down that ancient countryside, teaching and preaching and healing. Now this was to change.

Defeating evil through teaching and healing had not worked well enough. Jesus knew that he must take upon himself a more powerful, more sacrificial way.

He had warned his disciples that this moment would come, but they had not believed him. Now they sensed that he was about to face his greatest task. He must now come to mortal grips with the evil in this world, and in the battle he would try to destroy that evil. Evil could only be conquered through a powerful act, through a mighty struggle.

Where Does Evil Come From?

But why did evil exist in this world of God's? Those who have known God deepest and best (from whatever religion or culture) have found that God cares for human beings and that there is no ultimate maliciousness in God. They have found a God who longs and yearns over every human soul, giving whatever that soul needs in order to come to fullness and wholeness. This is what our direct experience of God is like.

But here on earth—an earth that is supposed to be God's creation—there is anything but this kind of treatment of human beings. Here there is our inhumanity to each other in war and murder and gossip and backbiting. There is nature's inhumanity to us in great catastrophes like the Bangladesh tidal wave in which hundreds of thousands of men, women, and children perished. And then there is the horror of physical illness in all its multitudinous forms. Certainly none of us needs to be reminded of how widespread such afflictions are in our world.

Where does the evil come from that afflicts us humans in so many ways, disrupting and defeating our lives? What is the source of this evil which Christ faced and conquered through so much suffering and agony? There is no completely satisfactory answer to this question. Or, to be more exact, there is no logical, no reasonable answer that is satisfactory. If this is God's world, why did he not make it so that evil could not enter? Why did he not make human beings so that they could grow up and develop without cutting their spiritual teeth on the evil in this world? Why. . . ?

A Deeper Answer

Although logic cannot give us a satisfactory answer to these questions, still there is a *more* than logical answer, a *more* than reasonable answer. We forget that we use two kinds of thinking. One is rational thinking, the logical analysis, which is so highly prized in our world and which, through science, has wrung so many secrets from the material world. But this is not the only way of thinking. Another kind exists, using images rather than ideas and concepts, with stories rather than with analyses. This is the thinking of mythology. ·

Again we must be reminded that myths are not untrue. *Rather, the myth expresses that which is so true and so near the heart of being that our logical thinking cannot touch this truth.* Myths express in images the reality of the nonphysical or spiritual world that is within us and surrounds us. Let's listen to this deeper level of our being as we ask why there is evil in God's world.

Probably we can find no better answer than the one found in the myth of Lucifer, referred to in various books of the Bible. We "cultured" people usually don't take such stories seriously, but this myth has something to tell us about evil. It says that evil came into our world because one element of God's creation rebelled and turned away from God. This was Lucifer—or Satan as he is better known to us.

Lucifer's Revolt

Lucifer was one of the great angels of heaven. He was even called the Son of the Morning or the Angel of Light. He was the brightest and best of the sons of the morning. He was endowed with more power and light and goodness than most of the other angels. His only fault was that there came a time when he looked around heaven and out into the universe and came to the logical conclusion that God wasn't doing the best possible job of running the world he had made. God was trying to run the universe with love, and that wasn't efficient.

This might not have been so bad in itself, but it brought Lucifer to the second logical conclusion: he could do a better job of running things than God. He felt that it was his duty to throw God out of heaven and rule in God's place.

Lucifer gathered around himself a group of dissatisfied angels who agreed that the loving and bungling kingship of God should be overthrown.

> And now war broke out in heaven, when Michael with his angels attacked the dragon. The dragon fought back with his angels, but they were defeated and driven out of heaven. The great dragon, the primeval serpent, known as the devil or Satan, who had deceived all the world, was hurled down to the earth and his angels were hurled down with him.
>
> —*Rev. 12:7–9*

In this way the myth of Lucifer shows that evil originated when something in God's world turned against God and revolted. This appears to be the actual source of evil. Real evil, malicious evil, is always a partial good, which pretends to be the whole good and acts as if it were the whole good. What made Satan so evil was the fact that he was so good to begin with.

Adam and Eve

In the next chapter of the myth of evil, Satan is established beneath the earth. Then God created the garden of Eden and placed Adam and Eve in it. At first they were perfectly happy. But one day Satan appeared in the guise of a serpent. He spoke to Eve and suggested that they should eat some fruit from the one tree that God had forbidden them to touch. Eve was afraid, but Satan only laughed. "Why, if you eat it," he reasoned, "you will become like gods yourselves!"

So Eve tasted the forbidden fruit and gave some to Adam. Then consciousness came to them, and, alas, with consciousness came pride. Adam discovered that he wanted to be like God. He wanted to run his own life rather than submit to God's way. And so evil broke into our world and has continued to plague human beings ever since.

When God confronted Adam with his disobedience, Adam blamed Eve. When Eve was confronted she blamed the serpent. Neither of them was willing to accept the burden of what they had done.

Joseph and Mary

There is an illuminating contrast in the way two others, Joseph and Mary, would later reverse this process of casting blame upon others. Mary accepted the gift of the child courageously, knowing what people would say, while Joseph trusted Mary and did not try to blame her. How differently Adam and Eve reacted.

From the first couple's pride and fear of being blamed, evil arose in the world. And from the second couple's humility, there arose a Savior capable of defeating and even destroying that evil.

Little more remains to be said about the origin of evil and how it broke into God's world than what is contained in this myth. Something high and holy turned against God, and this element has infected human beings and is still corrupting them. Evil is in God's world because Lucifer (or the Devil) turned against God and then persuaded human creatures to rebel, and he is still here among us bent on turning us away from God.

Life is a Warfare

Thus we humans are at war with ourselves within our own being. There is a part of us which hungers for God and a part which hungers only to satisfy itself and become God in its own right. One part of us longs to find its rest in God and is restless until we do. Another part of us fights against this feeling with all it is worth, saying into one's inner ear: "Look out for Number One. Take care of yourself. You can run your life better than God. Just live your own life and don't pay any attention to God."

And so we are torn and divided within ourselves. Like Paul we cry out,

> I cannot understand my own behavior. I fail to carry out the things I want to do, and I find myself doing the very things I hate. . . . I act against my own will. . . . What a wretched man I am! Who will rescue me from this body doomed to death?
>
> —*Romans 7:15,16,24*

Like Paul, we want to develop the fruits of the Spirit. Most people want their actions to bring love, peace, joy, forgiveness, patience, courage, humility, honesty, hope, faith. But too often they bring forth the fruits of darkness and evil. Too often our actions promote hate, guilt, fear, anxiety, tension, self-centeredness, selfishness, lust, cowardice, backbiting, gossip, or the like. And so we are often sick in soul and mind and body, for these things corrupt not only the soul but our minds and bodies as well. Thus the evil, which began in rebellion against God, still surrounds us in mental illness, neurosis, and physical sickness, as well as in war and murder, poverty, and marital conflict.

Victory in Jesus

But Paul did not conclude his cry of painful insight simply by declaring his wretchedness. He knew that Jesus had come to deal with evil. God in Christ had taken on the Evil One, and Jesus by his willingness to suffer and die had overcome the evil that originated from the pride and disobedience of Lucifer. Paul went on: "Thanks be to God through Jesus Christ our Lord!"

Thanks be to God indeed. Although there is evil in God's world, we need not remain bound to it because of what Jesus did as he turned his face to Jerusalem. Thanks be to God for the reality the church still offers.

> After saying this, what can we add? With God on our side who can be against us? Since God did not spare his own Son, but gave him up to benefit us all, we may be certain, after such a gift, that he will not refuse anything he can give. Could anyone accuse those that God has chosen? When God acquits, could anyone condemn? Could Christ Jesus? No! He not only died for us—he rose from the dead, and there at God's right hand he stands and pleads for us.
>
> Nothing therefore can come between us and the love of Christ, even if we are troubled or worried, or being persecuted, or lacking food or clothes, or being threatened or even attacked. . . . These are the trials through which we triumph, by the power of him who loved us.
>
> For I am certain of this: neither death nor life, no angel, no prince, nothing that exists, nothing still to come, nor any power, or height or depth, nor any created thing, can ever come between us and the love of God made visible in Christ Jesus our Lord.
>
> —*Romans 8:31–39*

7   To Love, To Console

There is an immense difference between knowing something with the head and knowing that same thing with the heart. (There is a similar difference between knowing something as an abstract idea and applying it to oneself.)

Suddenly a religious idea, which has been only irrelevant furniture in your mind, can become the central focus of life. The idea becomes alive, electric, and shoots through you. It is almost as if you become a part of the idea, as if you fuse with the living truth. Now you understand it from the inside.

I know exactly when the words that I will soon quote to you came alive for me. Flying home from a mission in the southeastern section of the United States, I had been alone since the early morning. I was on a small plane that swooped down onto little airstrips and gave me an imminent sense of eternity. Turned in upon myself, I was reflecting on the things that had happened during the week as I tried to lead a group of people further on the religious way.

Abruptly I realized that I was flying not too far from the home of my brother—with whom I was not in very good relationship. The next lap of the journey had taken me close to the home of my father and stepmother, with whom I was not in good relationship either. And on top of it, I was flying to see my daughter at the university. Since her early teens, our relationship had been strained also. A friend had suggested that I visit her in her own territory. I had phoned to say that I would stop over for five hours. Fortunately I did not know, as I was flying to see her, what she had said to her best friend after my call: "What will I do with father for five hours?"

St. Francis' Prayer

This was the situation that faced me as I was still and quiet, reflecting on me and my life. Then out of the depths of me bubbled the following words:

> O Divine Master,
> grant that I may not so much seek
> to be consoled—
>   as to console,
> to be understood—
>   as to understand
> to be loved—
>   as to love.

If you had asked me previously if I knew these words of St. Francis, I would have said that I did not. But a deeper level of me had received them and now brought them to the surface at the right moment.

All in a moment, I realized how much more often I had been seeking to be loved, understood and consoled than I had been seeking to give these things. Here I was, expecting brother, father, stepmother, and daughter to look out for my feelings and take care of me. When they didn't, the relationship failed.

It became clear to me that most of us human beings are more interested in being taken care of, in being loved, consoled and understood than in reaching out with these gifts to others— even members of our own families. How often parents are trying to get their children to satisfy their needs for sympathy and affection. How often adult children are still looking to their parents for support and strength.

And how frequently we complain: She did not speak to me or invite me to her party. He did not consider me a member of his group or did not pay proper attention to me. Our feelings are too easily hurt from too many causes, ranging from an imagined slur to an angry word or nasty action.

So much of this complaining would cease if we took seriously the words of St. Francis. And how could our wounded feelings persist if we were intent on bringing consolation and understanding to others instead of being overly concerned about us? How? It would be impossible.

Maturity

I also realized, there in the quiet of the plane, that emotional maturity only *begins* to take place in us when we begin giving rather than merely receiving. Children are interested only in themselves, in being loved and consoled and understood. This is a natural phase of development. To pass from childishness to adulthood, however, demands a shift toward giving these things rather than just receiving them. This is the essential mark of the real adult.

Until we can give love and understanding and consolation without any strings attached—without expecting anything in return—we are still emotional children, no matter how physically or intellectually grown up we are. Until we can give love, we are still immature, self-centred children.

During those hours in the plane I also saw that our real following of Jesus of Nazareth begins when we grasp the fact that it is more important to console and understand than to stretch out our hands to receive these things. It is not easy to give up our desire for satisfaction and attention. In fact, when we do something new comes to birth in us. If we proceed along this way, we lose our lives in order to gain them. As we live our St. Francis' prayer, we die and rise again. It is the way of the cross. When we try to live by this one little prayer, the whole gospel opens up. It comes to life. Suddenly the way of Christ begins to make sense.

The Sacrament of the Yellow Shoes

At this point in my reflections, the plane landed in Phoenix, Arizona. My daughter met me in her friend's car. I asked her where she would like to have lunch; she could pick any place she wanted to go. (She was not used to her clergyman father treating her in this way.) I took her to one of the loveliest resort hotels, where we sat beside the pool as the waiters hovered over us.

By now she had sensed that I had changed. Timidly she asked if I would like to go shopping in the Thomas Mall that afternoon. Frankly, that was not my idea of a Saturday afternoon in Phoenix, but I paused and remembered that I was there to love and console and understand. So I answered, "Myra, I would love to go shopping in the Thomas Mall.''

We went there. We walked up and back, up and back in that huge mall. Being interested in her and her reactions, I noted that our pace slackened in front of a certain shoe store. I also noticed that her eyes lighted upon a pair of yellow shoes. I said, ''Myra, would you like to try on those shoes?'' She thought that was a nice idea. Naturally they fitted perfectly. (That is known in theological language as ''divine providence.'') There was a yellow purse to match, and I asked her if she would like it, adding, ''My dear, this doesn't even come out of your allowance.'' This is known in theological language as grace.

Something happened that day between my daughter and me. Myra realized that I could be interested in her. No longer was it ''What will I do with father for five hours?'' but ''Why don't you come more often and stay longer?'' She knew now that I could see her just for herself.

I call this the Sacrament of the Yellow Shoes.

St. Francis

Amazing words, these words of St. Francis that strike at the heart of life and living. Even more amazing is the fact that the one who wrote them actually lived the way he wrote. Perhaps this is why they ring with such an authentic note, why they are so real. St. Francis of Assisi probably lived closer to the ideal of Christ than any one else has. So magnetic was his life that thousands of men and women began to follow him. Out of sheer necessity he founded the Franciscan Orders simply to organize his numerous disciples. In less than twenty years his life and the inspiration that flowed from him revitalized a dormant and cynical church. He did all this by the quality of his love.

Francis touched the hurt of life and ministered to the needs of the humblest of men and women. It is said that even the animals were drawn to him, and that he preached to the birds. He was more than an activist. He touched the deepest springs of life, and from them came visions and spiritual experiences of the most uncanny kind.

What is more, since he had been a renegade and dissolute rounder, his life gives hope even to the most lost and depraved person. His life says that it is never too late. He died at forty-four, but he had changed his world. Ever since his death, his example has continued to change lives—millions of them. The words that came to me on the plane were the central portion of what he called "A Simple Prayer."

Instruments of God's Peace

And what happens when we try to be more interested in loving and consoling and understanding than in being loved, consoled, and understood? We become instruments of God's peace in the world;

> Where there is hatred,
>   we sow love,
> where there is injury,
>   we bestow pardon,
> where there is doubt,
>   we bring faith,
> where there is despair,
>   we bring hope,
> where there is darkness,
>   we shed light,
> where there is weakness,
>   we inspire strength,
> and where there is
> sadness,
>   we bring joy.

All this flows naturally from the life that seeks to give rather than to receive. Such a life spreads love, pardon, faith, hope, light, strength, and joy. Inevitably!

And inwardly, when we live this way, we are filled, pardoned, and given eternal life, for it is in giving that we receive; it is in pardoning that we are pardoned; it is in dying that we are born to eternal life.

You can find the Prayer of St. Francis on beautifully illumined plaques or cards in most religious book shops. It is helpful to have one before you as a reminder that this was the way of St. Francis, and is the way of Jesus of Nazareth and the way of God the Divine Lover. In every household such a plaque could be a pointer toward the way to the world of Spirit, to God, to life. . . .

We cannot stop too often to meditate on these words, to let

our spirits drink of them, to mold our actions by them so that we *become these words* in heart and mind and soul and deed:

> O Divine Master,
> grant that I may not so much seek
> to be consoled—
>   as to console,
> to be understood—
>   as to understand,
> to be loved—as to love.

8   What Is Heaven Like?

Several weeks ago I was talking with a friend, once a student at the University of Notre Dame. He now teaches world religions at a small Catholic college. As we talked in depth, we shared our most vital concerns.

We agreed that it is impossible to study the religions of humankind without seeing a caring, organizing reality at the heart and center of the universe. We also agreed that in view of the poverty, oppression, hunger, and inner misery of a large part of the human race, life that does not extend beyond the grave becomes absurd, terrifying, and meaningless. One of the tasks of all genuinely religious people in the Western world is to share this vision of hope.

My friend and I disagreed in only one matter. My friend did not believe it possible to provide a meaningful picture of life after death; I believe that we can and need to give as clear a picture of eternal life as possible.

Let's see what we can do to provide an idea of the nature of heaven and afterlife. A big task for a few pages.

Balancing Earth and Heaven

At one time Christianity focused entirely too much on the life beyond death. The church avoided dealing with the agony of poverty and slavery by saying that everything would be balanced out, and all injustices would be set right on the other side. That was not the teaching or practice of Jesus of Nazareth.

We need to go out to the poor, the oppressed, the forgotten, the sick, the lonely. As Christians we need to do all we can to change the structures of society that crush and destroy human beings and create injustice.

We need to foster family life that gives birth to mature, caring, responsible people.

And we *also* need to offer each other a vision of that state of being that is called heaven, eternal life, afterlife. If we do not have this vision to share, we can leave the poor and broken in hopelessness and despair.

Unfortunately, many of us are afraid to look at the subject of heaven because it is necessary to look at death in the process. We live in a materialistic culture that is quite certain that life and hope and talents are extinguished at the grave. But life makes no sense if all we are is blotted out at death.

Pinchas Lapide is a Jew who survived the holocaust in Germany. His book, *The Resurrection of Jesus*, states that, of course, Jesus was raised from the dead; you can't account for the vital reality of the Early Church in any other way. Then he goes on with these profound words: "All honest theology is a theology of catastrophe, a theology that receives its impulse from the misery and nobility of our human nature."

Glimpses of the Beyond

It is possible to give some idea, some description of that state of being that exists on the other side of dying and death? I believe that we can. First of all, the glimpses that human beings have of eternal life have been exhaustively studied by a large group of doctors and psychologists. Most of these studies have been either ignored or rejected by theologians and the official church.

Raymond Moody's first study—*Life after Life*—brought the data out of the closet; he has continued his careful studies for thirteen years. In his last book, *The Light Beyond*, he abandons his tentative scientific attitude and writes: "I am convinced that people who have had near death experiences do get a glimpse of the beyond, a brief passage into a whole other reality."

Carl Jung wrote in his autobiography that his vision of his wife after her death was one of the most solid experiences of reality that he had ever encountered.

Jesus spoke several times specifically of life after death: in the story of Lazarus and the rich man, and in his response to the Pharisees who were trying to trip him up. To them he said that human beings were not married in heaven as on earth. But Jesus was talking about eternal life, the reign of God, the Kingdom of God, and the Kingdom of heaven all the time. We find some 328 references to God's reign or kingdom in the four Gospels, mostly on the lips of Jesus. Another 310 references to the reality of continuing fellowship with God in heaven are found in the other New Testament writings.

The Beatitudes

Jesus even gives a rather explicit description of the nature and quality of heaven in the Beatitudes. Jesus was describing those qualities of life that make us real human beings and bring us to the utter fulfillment of the Kingdom of heaven. As I was meditating on this passage, it came to me that the first and last statements ended the same way: "Blessed are the beggars in the spirit, for theirs is the Kingdom of heaven . . . Blessed are they who are persecuted for righteousness' sake, for theirs is the Kingdom of heaven." (Matt. 5:3 & 10). These two phrases form brackets around these six other descriptions of the quality of eternal life.

Quite obviously mourners do not always find comfort in this life and world; the meek do not often inherit the earth. The hungry for good often starve, and those who thirst for righteousness are often persecuted. The merciful often lose their shirts. The result for the single-minded and peacemakers is that they will see God and be called the children of God. These are heavenly gifts and experiences. Jesus was a realist and knew that a cross stood starkly before him.

Jesus was describing heaven in the last half of each of the infinitely profound Beatitudes. What is heaven according to Jesus of Nazareth? It is that eternal state of being where we are comforted and strengthened, made heirs of all earth's real treasures, and where we have our deepest longings filled and transformed into even deeper longings. In heaven we shall receive pardon and mercy and love and then know the utter joy of being an intimate part of the family of the loving God, working heavenly work and playing heavenly games.

Heaven is like a bud bursting into an eternal bloom, like a blossom ripening into an eternal fruit, like a train emerging from a dark tunnel into a glorious alpine valley. Heaven is the reality in which we find the kindly, humble, fine, noble, courageous, understanding, forgiving, striving, childlike, caring spirits whom we have loved on earth. Here we find fulfillment and consummation. This is home. We find confirmation of this vision of reality wherever we touch the deepest springs of life.

Our Younger Son's Death

These last years have been very difficult for my wife Barbara and for me. Several years ago our younger son was cut down by an untreatable encephalitis. We canceled all our engagements and went to him. We were his principle caretakers until he died on December third of 1988. Sitting by his bedside while he slept, I finished a book, *Reaching: The Journey to Fulfillment,* that he asked me to complete. One day as I sat there in silent, deep mutual communion, the following words came to me. They seemed to be his words. Later, when I shared them with him, he asked me for a copy, which he shared with a mutual friend, saying, "Father understands how I feel."

> Fear not for me. I'm not afraid.
> A new adventure awaits me,
> A new, more brilliant being
> Is about to birth
> Into a different place and time.
> The garden of heaven and those abiding there
> Are calling me insistently. They want me soon.
> They sing of my courage and frustration,
> Of years of seeking, restless searching . . .
> So many roads that petered out
> In scorching desert and burning sand
> And still I kept on, was guided.
> Those voices promise
> To answer all my questions
> With love abounded, limitless.
> They offer intimacy, closeness, far richer
> Then I had dared to hope for, and wisdom, too,
> And living water drawn from the deepest well
> That holds the secret mysteries safe
> From vain and curious wanderers.
> The voices also sing of love and loving,
> Of giving all I had and only at this moment
> Knowing that my arrow struck its mark.

> Do not hold me back. I'll be with you still
> In fuller measure than I've ever been before.
>
> The sun is rising from the sea
> As one by one the stars are lost in light.
> The broken has been mended.
> I can be loved and love.
> It is time to go.
> Pushed beyond the limits
> Of death and pain and hope.
> I find the real, Eternal Love.

And how do we let go of our beloved and still let them know how much we miss and love them? How do we stay within the communion of saints that transcends space and time? Barbara and I were moved to write a prayer that we often say, particularly at our daily Eucharist. We modeled it on one that Alan Paton printed in his tribute to his wife—*For You, Departed.*

A Prayer for the Departed

O Mother-Father God, ever loving and ever living, the final reality in which all souls find their completion, rest, and fulfillment, we pray for him whom you know and love far more deeply than we can ever imagine. Give him your light and love for which he sought so fervently. In your mercy, heal, strengthen, enlighten, and guide him as he enters the unbounded and mysterious vistas of eternity. May his immortal being reveal more and more the infinite potential with which you endow the human soul. May he know the intimate fellowship of the children of God and become an ambassador of your caring and peace to all dimensions of your universe.

O Gracious One, let him know how much we love and miss his physical presence and long to be with him. Grant that he may be allowed to guide and guard our journey until we meet in that condition where partings cease. Until then give us a sense of his loving presence. Heal all the wounds inflicted by an insensitive and unconscious society. Let us minister in any way we can to his growth, peace, and joy. Let us do nothing that keeps us from fellowship together in the communion of saints. We ask this of you, a loving God who created us, saw our misery, came among us, suffered with us, suffered for us, and by rising again opened to us the portals of eternal life. Amen.

9   The Practical Importance of Heaven

The evidence continues to pour in from every side. Human consciousness is not extinguished at death like a candle being snuffed out. However, the most impressive studies, and the most scientific, have occurred in the last few years. Dr. Kenneth Ring, a University of Connecticut psychologist intrigued by the accounts given by Dr. Raymond Moody, has presented a much more careful and balanced study of the fact that many people come to the point of clinical death and return to describe remarkably similar experiences. Another doctor, Michael Sabom, in his careful study *Recollections of Death: A Medical Investigation*, reveals that the author started as a skeptic and ended writing a confirmation that human knowing continues even when the body and brain have ceased functioning. Other studies show how frequently the living are encountered by the deceased—even Billy Graham refers to this experience.

The most interesting thing about this data is how seldom it is discussed among theologians and academic Christians. Some theologians seem to have an actual hostility to this data and feel that Christian belief in eternal life should be based upon faith alone. Other influential Christian thinkers cast doubt on the existence of any meaningful continuance of human consciousness or state that we can be perfectly good Christians without any hope of any life beyond the grave. Naturally such writers offer no hint of what that life might be. One reason that I wrote my book, *Afterlife: The Other Side of Dying*, was to show that this new data confirms and strengthens the vision of Christ and his Church about the life beyond death. This teaching of Jesus about life after death is integral to the good news and has a host of very practical implications for living life and the Christian life in particular.

Many people do not take seriously either the data that scientists have been accumulating or the picture of the Church about afterlife. One reason for this is that many of us are caught in a materialistic world view and so we have no place in our thinking for any existence that is not physical. It is very difficult to perceive what we do not expect to see as Postman and Bruner have demonstrated in the cognitive learning laboratory at Harvard. They painted a six of spades red just as if it were the six of diamonds or hearts and reinserted it in a deck of cards. The deck was then shown to subjects. Almost none of them ''saw'' the red six of spades as it was.

There is a lot of other evidence that people perceive with difficulty data that is anamalous and does not fit into their world view. If this is true of physical sensations, how much more true of data that cannot be explained in terms of the five senses. Until we have a place in our scheme of things for spiritual reality, we are not going to accept the medical evidence for continuing life after death or take seriously the picture that the church presents. Unfortunately, many Christian thinkers and many Christians have drunk so deeply of the materialism of our time that they have lost their convictions about the afterlife.

What Is Heaven Like?

The early church had a very vivid belief and experience of the kingdom of heaven being close at hand. Early Christians believed Jesus when he taught that we could enter that kingdom now to some degree and step into it forever at death. They had a clear image of what that life would be. In large measure because of this conviction they outlived, outfought, and outdied the ancient world and conquered that world. The same conviction continued in the Christian church right up through the sixteenth century. At times this belief became too concrete, but it was real. Then came the skepticism and materialism of the next centuries and Christian belief in afterlife eroded away.

We need a clear, sensible, and understandable view of life after death if Christians are to live full Christian lives. Vague suggestions are not enough. In *Afterlife*, I tried to provide such a picture. In the last pages of Thomas Wolfe's *You Can't Go Home Again*, we find these words: "To lose the earth you know, for greater knowing; to lose the life you have, for greater life; to leave the friends you loved, for greater loving; to find a land more kind than home, more large than earth. . . . Whereon the pillars of this earth are founded, toward which the conscience of the world is tending . . . a wind is rising, and the rivers flow." Here is a concrete picture. Jesus was even more specific as we have shown in our last meditation. This is the kingdom to which we ask God to bring us when we pray: "Thy kingdom come . . ."

The Practical Results of Belief

Heaven, then, is the simultaneous fruition of life without bounds as one ancient Christian wrote. How different our daily life in the here and now becomes when death offers such a consummation of life. The vision of the future flows back and changes the present just as the setting sun sets the eastern sky aflame. Let's look at the many ways that our attitudes and concerns are changed.

First of all, once we realize the nature of the kingdom toward which we are all moving inevitably, we will want to prepare for the journey. Few travelers set off for an extended visit to a strange land without finding out all they can about the place to which they are going. What kind of clothes and shoes do we need? What are the customs of the people? Some will even try to learn a little of the language. And, if we are immigrating to a new country, the only sensible approach is to know all we can about the climate and the people who live there.

Once we have concluded that we are going to be immigrants to the kingdom of which Jesus spoke, where the Love reigns, we will want to find out all we can about that place and prepare ourselves so that we can often fit in there. We will try to shape our lives to the customs and attitudes that we will find. If we can have some previews of what life is going to be, if we can spend some time with those who are citizens there, we would be very foolish not to do so. Jesus said that we could have some experiences of the kingdom now and these would help us shape our lives. We will spend time in prayer and meditation and reading scripture; we will try to be forgiving and caring in all relationships; we will reach out to the needy and unfortunate, the prisoners and the sick.

Then a vision of heaven will give strength to many people to carry on. Many people lead very unsatisfactory lives—they have suffered oppression, political slavery, poverty, and disaster. They have been crippled by physical or psychological deformity, as well as blasted by prejudice and war and rejection. For these people this life is a bad joke unless there is something more, unless they can find the comfort of Abraham's bosom. So often we, who live in a comfortable land where the poor are rich by the standards of some nations, forget that a third of the world's children go to bed hungry every night and millions die unattended and forgotten.

For many people life is miserable and unfair, and the idea of reincarnation offers only more of the same. It is the comfortable people who seem to long for reincarnation. I personally hope I can make it through this life once and then abide within Abba's mercy and love. Only a kingdom such as Jesus described can compensate for what many of us suffer here, both psychologically and physically.

How can the miserable of the earth have hope and courage to fight on through unless there is something to hope for? Jesus speaks of the ultimate value of every human being. This only makes sense when hurting humankind is comforted and filled and given mercy at some point. The good news of Jesus is that there is such a culmination to life. This is essential to his message of the incredible love of the prodigal Abba in heaven for each of us.

Without the fruition of life in eternity, as Jesus described it, the love of God loses its meaning and power. Love, which loves for a time and lets us dry up and blow away, is no love at all. Karl Jaspers has written that we achieve immortality to the extent that we love. Love and everlasting life are intertwined with one another. Can the heart and center of this universe be self-giving love for you and me it if allows us to be snuffed out and live unfulfilled lives at that?

If this God we have sometimes known in our deepest, best moments is not love, then our will to love one another has its foundation torn away. It is hard for us to love the enemy and the stranger and sometimes even those close to us. Sometimes I can only summon up the strength to love as I reflect upon that love which never fails to reach out to me, and that love loses its very meaning if there is no afterlife. A central dynamic of vital Christianity is then lost.

The Disaster of Losing Meaning

Those who see the grave as the final goal of life, who believe that this is all that life offers, are robbed of meaning and significance. And when life's value consists only in what earth offers, then material things become more and more central; the struggle for possession of these objects becomes more intense, and the worst of human nature is stimulated. These material possessions, once obtained, usually turn to dust and ashes; futility and emptiness then surrounds our deaths.

Those who do not succeed in the struggle are driven to despair. It is thin comfort that our influence for good may linger on and touch the lives of those who come after us. Some of those who view the grave as final try to forget extinction and try to lose themselves in busyness or in the oblivion of alcohol and drugs and crude pleasures.

There are however, many who can't repress and so forget the secular belief that life ends with our death. Those of us who cannot escape facing a meaningless death must battle with the spectres of fear and hate, of depression and stress. These devastating emotions destroy not only the mind, but the body as well.

Fear is a normal reaction to threat, and what is more threatening than finding that we are not deeply related to this world in which we live and are cast away at death as useless husks. This is the flight response. There are others who respond to threat with anger and attack and hatred. This is the fight response which sometimes smoulders like a low unquenchable fire and sometimes breaks out in violence and destructiveness. How much our world suffers from this reaction to meaningless existence—in war, street violence, and race hatred. Then, too, there is stress. When we believe that we are alien creatures in a world that holds no destiny for us, then we must do everything for ourselves, by our effort, struggle, striving. How intolerable and destructive this stress can be.

In these emotions we can struggle to hide or destroy or build impregnable castles for ourselves. In depression our inner stance collapses and we fall into the cesspool deep within our inner being—rebuilding seems hopeless. All is lost and even the struggle has lost its meaning.

We are not quite bright if we look toward meaninglessness extinction and do not have one of these reactions. These are the normal and natural reactions to meaninglessness. Carl Jung reminds us that loss of meaning is a *sickness* and causes physical illness as well as emotional distress.

Beset with fear, anger, and stress the body summons all its resources. The ductless glands pour out energizers—the heart pounds, the blood pressure rises, blood sugar is released and mixes with the oxygen to give us an extra spurt of energy. Even the blood clotting time goes down to prepare for possible wounds. This is an appropriate reaction for a cave person faced with an attacking tiger. The identical response is triggered by nothing more than the threat of living in a world with no purpose and of slipping into a dark and random void at death. When these threatening reactions are continued indefinitely, they literally dynamite the physical body wreaking havoc on heart and blood vessels, digestion, and nearly every other bodily function.

Overcome by depression, the body gives up along with the soul. The natural resistance of the body deteriorates—the white blood cells are no longer vigilant against invaders. We are open to infection and even cancer as the Simmontons show in their book *Getting Well Again*. Those who have a sense of their ultimate value and their place in the universe can withstand the tensions of life creatively and turn them into victory. This is nearly impossible unless we see life as stretching beyond the grave. If lack of meaning is so alien to life, it well might be against the grain of all things.

Heaven as Fulfillment

As life unfolds before me, I realize how poor in spirit I am and how far I have to go. The more my religious life grows and develops, the more I try to pray and care and love, the greater I perceive the mountain before me which I seek to climb. I realize that I cannot by my own effort become what I know I need to become. Far from being discouraged I realize that I am in good company as all the saints complained that they were but beginners on the spiritual journey—the religious quest. At the end of a long life, I am just beginning. I need transformation after transformation and resurrection after resurrection to become what God has in mind for me.

How utterly futile my life is if I am cut off at that point, if there is no afterlife in which to complete what I have begun. Then the intimations of the kingdom, which I have known in the silence waiting upon the risen Christ, and the love, which I have experienced in my deepest moments of relationship with God and human beings, are both illusion. My growing comes to an end not even with a bang, but only with a whimper. Without the kingdom on the other side of dying, my religious quest is really quite stupid and vain.

One reason that many people deny the afterlife is because they do not want to be saddled with the responsibility of their own eternal destiny. Being alone by themselves with nothing to do can be a terror for many people and is the worst punishment for prisoners. Having to bear their own empty inner beings alone is more than some people can face. Denial of an afterlife can be a materialistic cop out for those who fear to face the continuing reality of their substantial souls.

Afterlife and the Resurrection

It is difficult for most of us to imagine a land "more large" than earth and more kind than home. The problem has been with us a long time. Paul wrote to the Corinthians to correct the error of some of them who believed that the dead did not rise.

> For if the dead are not raised, neither has Christ been raised. And if Christ has not been raised, then your faith is a delusion and you are still lost in your sins. It would also mean that the believers in Christ who have died are lost. If our hope in Christ is good for this life only, and no more, then we deserve more pity than anyone else in all the world.
>
> —1 Cor. 15:16–19 in *Good News for Modern Man*

Without continuing life beyond death those who were persecuted for Christ's sake were tragically deluded people.

The resurrection of Jesus is far more than an assurance of life after death; it is the evidence that the powers of evil and darkness have been defeated through self-giving love. If we look back before the dawn of time and space, we will find in the center of divine reality the incredible love that Jesus portrayed in dying for us while we were still in our rebellion and lostness. The resurrection is the clue through which we discover this treasure.

It is perfectly obvious to any of us who look at the plight of our neighbours in this global community, that this love does not achieve its goals on earth with all the help we give or in spite of all the hindrance we offer. Unless there is life beyond the grave where this love can have its way, then the resurrection of Jesus is a vain gesture and practicing Christians deserve more pity than anyone else in all the world.

The Christian mission is a desire to share the hope, joy, and victory of Christ with the world. In recent years the ardor of this mission has cooled. Unless there is life after death, we have but little to offer our hurt and broken world. We have no gospel, no good news, no comfort. With the victory of Jesus on the cross and with a vision of coming home to the kingdom of the Divine Lover when this life is over, we are empowered to go out and save men and women and nations overwhelmed by the storms raging across our world. Only the perverse among us will fail to offer to the hurting world the infinite hope that opens up for everyone through Jesus' resurrection.

10   He Is Risen, Alleluia!

Sometime early Easter morning, Jesus rose from the dead.

On Friday he had truly died as any other person dies, but now he was dead no longer.

The witnesses were many—the women who found the empty tomb, Mary Magdalen to whom he revealed himself in the garden, the two disciples on the way to Emmaus, and the eleven disciples gathered fearfully in the Upper Room. For forty days he continued to appear to those closest to him, until in a burst of glory he disappeared from their sight. Then, these broken, ineffective, cowardly men and women went out to conquer the Roman Empire—and conquer it they did.

What Did They See?

What does it mean that Jesus was raised from the dead and appeared to these people? What did they experience? What happened to them in this experience that changed their lives? What did they see?

Was it only a ghost? Today, many don't believe in such things as ghosts, the tenuous, shade-like appearances of the dead, although they have been attested to over the centuries. No, Jesus could not have appeared as a ghost. There is always something pathetic in a ghost. It has no power other than to utter a few noises and perhaps to warn or terrify those whom it visits. The ghosts in *Hamlet* and *Macbeth* are typical examples of the general description. Also, ghosts don't transform lives. They don't make anyone happy. There is nothing victorious in a ghost, nothing triumphant. Certainly the people who saw Jesus were not encountering a ghost.

What, then, did they see? Perhaps it was a resuscitated body. Since the Gospels say that he ate fish with them, the body had to be physical in appearance. But there are other Gospel examples of persons being raised from the dead: Lazarus, Jairus' daughter, the son of the widow of Naim. These people attracted some attention, but no one shaped a religion around them. What would have been so transforming if Jesus' physical body had merely resumed life?

What the disciples saw on that first Easter morning was not just a ghost or a revived body. What they saw was something *entirely new*. Here was a physical body that was so shot through with spiritual reality that the two met and merged. It was the familiar physical body of Jesus, which they recognized, but it was transformed and permeated with spiritual power. His body had become the meeting point of heaven and earth, in which all of earth's reality was present as well as all of heaven's glory. Matter and energy are not as far apart as was once believed. Spirit and body are not as separated as once thought. Here in the Risen Christ was all the reality of the earth and all the glory and power of God and heaven. Thus this body could obey the laws of matter *and* the laws of the spirit. Jesus could eat a meal and have Thomas place his hand in his side, and at the same time he could disappear in a moment and ascend to heaven in a blaze of glory.

A New Creation

Truly, in the resurrected body of Jesus, we have a new creation, a new reality: the merging of the physical and the spiritual, the transfiguration of the physical with the spirit. The two meet and mingle. The meaning and secret of life is felt and known, even though it is not understood.

Those who experienced this reality were brought into contact with the center and source of all reality. They knew the Holy. They knew God. Their lives were simply remade as they grasped the meaning of life, or rather were grasped by it. They were no longer ordinary people. The Spirit who had transfigured Jesus had touched and transformed them also. St. Paul exults in this new dimension of life: ''. . . if anyone is in

Christ, that person is a new creation. The old order had passed
away; now all is new!'' (II Cor. 5:17).

This experience of the new reality did not cease with Christ's
ascension. In the first century, Saul of Tarsus was radically
changed into Paul through his meeting with the glorified
Messiah on the road to Damascus. Centuries later, Francis of
Assisi experienced so great a union with the risen Lord that his
very body took on the characteristics of Christ's—the stigmata.
The lives of the saints are replete with testimonies to the living
presence of the resurrected Christ in all ages. Even today,
countless men and women are motivated to heroic deeds as a
result of a profound personal awareness of Jesus in their lives.
They say with Paul, ''This is the Christ we proclaim . . . hoping
to make everyone complete in Christ. For this I work and
struggle, impelled by that energy of his which is so powerful a
force within me.'' (Col. 1:28–29).

However, we must be careful not to imagine that such
experiences are limited to the great saints of the past and
present. Although the manner of the experiences may vary in
clarity and intensity, the transforming touch of the risen Christ
is possible for each Christian. We need only open our lives to
him and have the courage to risk an encounter with our glorified
Lord.

How Do We See?

A careful reading of the resurrection narratives gives us some
insight into several dispositions of heart which are necessary to
experience the Christ. For example, Mary Magdalen met the
risen Lord in the garden, but on account of her tears she could
not tell that he was not the gardener (John 20:10–18). When he
spoke her name, however, she immediately recognized him.
Mary was the one who had loved so much because she had been
forgiven much. So, through her love, she found new life in
Jesus. We, too, can love as Mary did if only we allow ourselves
to do so.

> We, for our part, love
> because he first loved us.
> —I John 4:19

All we know about the two men on the road to Emmaus is that

they were talking about Jesus and the events of Good Friday as they journeyed (Luke 24:13–15). This was their concern, their interest. Their minds and their hearts were full of Jesus and what he meant. When the Lord appeared, they did not recognize him; nevertheless, their hearts soon burned within them. We, too, can have our hearts and minds so centered on the redeeming Lord, that suddenly he will be with us and our hearts will burn within us and we will recognize him. So it was with St. Francis. So it must be with us. "Those who live according to the flesh are intent on the things of the flesh, those who live according to the spirit, on those of the spirit." (Rom. 8:5).

The other disciples laughed at the message of the women. They thought that Mary Magdalen was out of her mind, yet they gathered together in the Upper Room and faithfully persevered. They had no hope, no confidence, but they had loyalty and obedience. They did not give up. Then, suddenly, he was in their midst.

Likewise, as we gather together faithfully in Christian community and worship, sometimes perhaps wondering why we do it but giving it our best, suddenly he is with us too and we know the reality of the risen Christ. It is noteworthy that rarely, very rarely, does he ever appear to the pagan, doubting world. Faithfulness is an essential. In his first epistle, St. Peter exhorts his readers to strengthen their faith by focusing on the promise:

> There is cause for rejoicing here. You may for a time have to suffer the distress of many trials; but this is so that your faith, which is more precious than the passing splendor of fire-tried gold, may by its genuineness lead to praise, glory, and honor when Jesus Christ appears. Although you have never seen him, you love him, and without seeing you now believe in him, and rejoice with inexpressible joy touched with glory because you are achieving faith's goal, your salvation.
>
> —I Pet. 1:6–9

So, here we see three vital conditions for recognizing the risen Christ in our lives—love, interest, and fidelity.

Yesterday, Today and Forever

The risen Christ is still in our midst. But perhaps he is waiting for the right moment of our love and concern and dedication before he breaks through and touches us with that hope and transformation for which we all long. In recent years, through the charismatic, Cursillo, and other renewal movements, many of us have experienced the risen Christ in a new and life-changing way. It is important for us to press on in the way of love, interest, and fidelity, since our union with Christ cannot be a once-and-for-all experience. In a certain sense, each day is a new life. We should be open to a continual transformation of our lives as Christ meets us in each new moment, each new circumstance.

The Lord has promised that those who seek will find. May Paul's words be our own:

> I wish to know Christ and the power flowing from his resurrection; likewise to know how to share in his sufferings by being formed into the pattern of his death. Thus do I hope that I may arrive at resurrection from the dead.''
>
> —Phil. 3:10–12

Epilogue to Part Two

We have been looking at a very serious subject—the death and resurrection of the finest human being who ever lived. We have seen victory emerge out of defeat and annihilation. Jesus was not always serious. Not only did he show joy, he also had a wonderful sense of humor and some of his stories, like the prodigal son and the unjust steward, are shot through with humor. The matter of death is a very painful one and needs a lighter touch as well as a more serious one.

One of my closest friends, and former parishioner, sent me the following poem that she found among her mother's papers after her death. Whether her mother wrote it or not I do not know, but here it is:

> I dreamed death came the other night
> And heaven's gate swung wide.
> With kindly grace, an angel ushered me inside.
> And there, to my astonishment,
> Stood folk I'd known on earth—
> Some I'd judged and labeled as
>   "Unfit" or "Little Worth."
> Indignant words rose to my lips
>   but never were set free,
> For every face showed stunned surprise . . .
> No one expected *me*!

One of the most beautiful letters I ever received came from a minister who had fought a valiant battle against leukemia. These words are Howard Crenshaw's final greeting to his friends:

A pastor friend called a few days ago and asked how I was doing. My initial thought was to tell him, "It looks like I'm going downhill." Then an insight came to me, and I said to him, "I was about to tell you I'm going downhill, but what I want to say is: I'm going uphill; I'm climbing Jacob's ladder."

One morning shortly after that I was lying in bed letting my mind think about that climb. The idea became clearer to me and I began to see life in terms of climbing a mountain. For those who have hiked in the mountains, this concept will be more understandable. When we start the climb, we no sooner reach a peak than we discover there are more peaks ahead separating us with valleys, cliffs, and meadows, which have to be crossed. Sometimes they are beautiful and easy. Other times they are tough and require a struggle, but one keeps on traveling.

Then I began to see myself on this mountain and could imagine myself approaching the final peak. I was not alone, not only was God with me, but also my family and a host of friends, and then I realized there would come that time when I would have to turn loose of family and friends and finish the climb without them. While sharing this with my family, we were intensely aware of the pain that's involved in that final separation. However, we know that we are never fully separated because the God who will walk with me to the final peak and the glory that lies beyond, will be the same God who will be present with my family and friends.

Today is Easter. We just celebrated the resurrection Eucharist in our own living room because of the illness of a member of the family and we wanted to be together. The framework for the huge east window of this room makes a more than life-sized cross. Beyond the window, redwoods and madrones remind us of the everlastingness of life. As we began our service, I thought of Howard Crenshaw and my deceased son John and many others who have died and passed on to the other side of the communion of saints; and then I read the words of the great Easter hymn:

> The strife is o'er, the battle done,
> The victory of life is won;
> The song of triumph has begun.
> Alleluia!

> The powers of death have done their
> worst,
> But Christ their legions hath dispersed:
> Let shout of holy joy outburst.
> Alleluia!